I N   A C T I O N

Recruiting and Retaining Call Center Employees

ELEVEN

CASE STUDIES

FROM THE

REAL WORLD

OF TRAINING

JACK J. PHILLIPS
SERIES EDITOR

NATALIE L. PETOUHOFF
EDITOR

ASTD
*Linking People,
Learning & Performance*

Ordering information: Books published by ASTD can be ordered by calling 800.628.2783 or 703.683.8100, or via the Website at www.astd.org.

Library of Congress Catalog Card Number: 2001087854

ISBN: 1-56286294-4

Table of Contents

Introduction to the *In Action* Series

Like most professionals, the people involved in HRD are eager to see practical applications of models, techniques, theories, strategies, and issues relevant to their field. In recent years, practitioners have developed an intense desire to learn about the firsthand experiences of organizations implementing HRD programs. To fill this critical void, the Publishing Review Committee of ASTD established the *In Action* casebook series. Covering a variety of topics in HRD, the series significantly adds to the current literature in the field.

The *In Action* series objectives are as follows:

- *To provide real-world examples of HRD program application and implementation.* Each case describes significant issues, events, actions, and activities. When possible, actual names of organizations and individuals are used. Where names are disguised, the events are factual.
- *To focus on challenging and difficult issues confronting the HRD field.* These cases explore areas where it is difficult to find information or where processes or techniques are not standardized or fully developed. Emerging issues critical to success are also explored.
- *To recognize the work of professionals in the HRD field by presenting best practices.* Each casebook represents the most effective examples available. Issue editors are experienced professionals, and topics are carefully selected to ensure that they represent important and timely issues. Cases are written by highly respected HRD practitioners, authors, researchers, and consultants. The authors focus on many high-profile organizations—names you will quickly recognize.
- *To serve as a self-teaching tool for people learning about the HRD field.* As a stand-alone reference, each volume is a practical learning tool that fully explores numerous topics and issues.
- *To present a medium for teaching groups about the practical aspects of HRD.* Each book is a useful supplement to general and specialized HRD textbooks and serves as a discussion guide to enhance learning in formal and informal settings.

These cases will challenge and motivate you. The new insights you gain will serve as an impetus for positive change in your organization. If you have a case that might serve the same purpose for other HRD professionals, please contact me. New casebooks are being developed. If you have suggestions on ways to improve the *In Action series*, your input will be welcomed.

Jack J. Phillips
In Action Series Editor
P.O. Box 380637
Birmingham, AL 35238-0637
phone: 205.678.8038
fax: 205.678.0177
email: serieseditor@aol.com

Preface

Trainers have understood for a very long time that recruiting the right people with the right skills and providing them with great training is the key to creating a great business. With the advent of measurement and return-on-investment calculations for these key business activities comes the acknowledgement from all facets of business professionals that performance management does make a difference to profits, sales, and customer satisfaction. As trainers, HR professionals and managers learn the language to explain how business is affected, the more focus (time, energy, and resources) can be placed on them without the typical resistances of the past. This book provides information about training, recruiting, and evaluating programs that you can use as models and guides. In addition, we have included cases on process and technology to provide a full range of options in creating your call center solution.

Need for This Book

This casebook provides numerous examples of performance management programs in diverse applications. One basic premise remains constant in all of the applications: People matter most, and, when they adopt a relationship-based leadership style, the workplace becomes successful. Performance management involves all willing participants creating a learning environment together.

With a company's need to recruit and keep the best talent, performance management is its best strategy for remaining competitive in the global marketplace in which employees have more choices than ever before. As illustrated by the cases in this book, performance management is used to improve both personal and organizational skills. The primary purpose of this book is to illustrate the various ways people can reach their potential and thereby contribute to the bottom line, making all more profitable by creating stronger and more stable companies that can offer higher wages and excellent benefit packages. A company's success is the employee's success.

Target Audience

CEOs, chief operating officers (COOs), and general managers as well as human resource managers and training and development specialists will find the information in this book helpful in strategically planning new programs in their organizations or in strengthening and expanding their existing development programs. External and internal knowledge management consultants will be able to point to the techniques of some of the pioneers to design programs to preserve the knowledge and skills for the next generation of workers. Team leaders and coaches will find successful recruiting, training, and evaluation techniques and activities. These cases can also be used in human resource development classes at universities and colleges as discussion for best practices.

The Cases

The most difficult part of developing this publication was in deciding which cases to use because the topic of training, recruiting, and evaluation is so wide reaching. We tried to provide a variety of applications to appeal to all audiences. In addition, we wanted to offer technology and process solutions as well as the standard chapters. The chapters on benchmarking should help with the implementation and measurement as readers begin to make changes to their current programs.

Case Authors

The case authors for this book represent a wide spectrum of knowledge and expertise in the field of consulting, performance management, and coaching. Some are widely known in their fields, and you will immediately recognize their names. Some are newer contributors to the field. Some are well known in other areas of HRD yet their chapter makes valuable contributions to this popular and fast-growing field. Collectively these authors represent a stunning amount of talent, knowledge, and expertise, which they have willingly shared with us in these cases. All are experienced practitioners, as you will see once you read their cases. It has been a great pleasure for me to work with all of these case authors, some old friends and colleagues and others new friends and colleagues.

Acknowledgements

I would like to thank the authors of the cases for the time and effort they put into them. I have learned a lot from working with each individual author, and the programs they have developed have enriched my understanding and appreciation for this field. I also want to thank the organizations, companies, and individuals who have graciously allowed the use of their names and details of their programs for this publication. I am grateful to the American Society of Training & Development; Series Editor Jack Phillips; and Patti Phillips, Kelly Perkins, and Joyce Alff of the Chelsea Group for this opportunity. I owe a special thanks to Joyce for keeping me on schedule, despite all the issues that came up.

Finally I wish to thank all my friends and family that were so patient during the writing of the case study book and for their support and understanding. Especially fun for me was working with my sister, Tanya, who wrote one of the cases studies. And I want to acknowledge the management team at www.BenchmarkPortal.com and Jon Anton, who allowed me to work on this book as a contribution to the field of performance management, call centers, and human potential.

Natalie L. Petouhoff
Santa Monica, CA
December 2001

How to Use This Casebook

This book presents cases with a variety of approaches for recruiting, training, and evaluating call center employees as well as cases on business processes and technology. The chapter on benchmarking provides a way to determine the "as is" and "could be" states of your organization to maximize performance and reduce costs. Most of the cases deal with recruiting in some fashion, several of the cases describe training programs in organizations, two cases deal with technology and process, and one case describes benchmarking practices in call centers. Several of the chapters talk about the use of assessments in the recruiting and training process. Each case describes different strategies and approaches to improving human performance and promoting lifelong learning, retention, and increased productivity. The cases offer a wide range of settings representing sales organizations, financial services organizations, a power company, airline ticket sales, and private individuals. The cases represent practices of leading consultants, educators, coaches, practitioners, and researchers in the fields of mentoring and coaching. Table 1 provides an overview of the cases. It provides descriptions of the cases in the order that they appear in the book and should be useful as a quick reference source for readers.

Prepared by practitioners in the field, the cases are a rich source of information in the field of recruiting, training, and evaluating call center employees. Each case does not specifically represent the ideal approach to each situation. Part of the lifelong learning process is continuous reflection and improvement. Each case presents teaching questions designed to stimulate discussion and encourage the reader to analyze the cases, understand the issues, and suggest improvements. Many of these cases represent programs that have undergone quality improvements since their first implementation.

Using the Cases

There are several ways to use this book. It will be helpful to anyone interested in recruiting, training, or evaluating employees. This applies to HRD consultants, practitioners, organizational managers,

Table 1. Overview of case studies by industry, programs, and target audience.

Case	Industry	HRD Program	Target Audience
Health-Care Corporation	Health care	Management/HR consulting	HRD professionals, business, industry
Edcor	Call center operations services	Managing and operating call centers—people and technology	HRD professionals, business, industry, government
Intuit	Software and Internet financial services	Recruiting and training	HRD professionals, business, industry, education, sales associates
Wireless Voice and Data Service Company	Wireless voice and data services	Measuring training effectiveness	HRD professionals, business, industry, government
Trans American Airways	Airline	Mentoring in education and connecting with business	Education, HRD professionals, business, industry
Data and Voice Communication Service Company	Data and voice communication services	Training through call simulations	HRD professionals, business, training staffs
Duke Power	Electric utility services	Self-directed training	Training professionals, HRD professionals, government, business, industry
Financial Institution	Financial services	Call center benchmarking and ROI	HRD professionals, government, business, industry

Braun Consumer Service Center	Consumer products	Dealing with the human aspect of change	Training professionals, HRD professionals, business, industry
Financial Services Company	Financial services	Recruiting, training, and retaining via holistic means	HRD professionals, government, business, industry
Purdue University	Customer service	Using selection benchmark to increase customer service	HRD professionals, government, business, industry

educators, and researchers. The reader can read the cases, analyze the processes described in each application, and choose the pieces that are helpful.

This book will be useful in training sessions, with the cases serving as a basis for discussion. HRD professionals will find these cases useful for comparison of current practices in mentoring programs and the different perspectives presented. Because the cases are based on real-life situations, the outcomes can provide valuable data for program planning.

This book can also supplement other training and development textbooks. Each case contains discussion questions to optimize its use in a seminar format.

Follow-Up

Each case author has suggested questions that can be used to initiate discussion; however, feel free to suggest questions of your own. Each case is unique. What has worked well for one organization may not work well for another. It is not the intention of this book that the readers simply seek to duplicate the approaches presented here. However, the book does provide a rich variety of strategies and suggestions from which to adapt one's own approach.

To provide a variety of cases, it was necessary to limit the length of the cases, and some cases may be shorter than both the authors and the editors might prefer. If additional information on a case is needed, the lead author may be contacted directly via the email or street address at the end of each case.

Tools to Increase Human Potential and the Bottom Line

Natalie L. Petouhoff

In the past, decision makers and stakeholders did not understood that there is a connection between human potential and a company's profit. Even if leaders had a sense that there was a connection, they did not know what to do about it. This chapter is to help anyone in a call center increase the effectiveness of the selection, recruitment, training, and development processes by providing a new business paradigm and tools that increase human performance. This chapter describes the tools fully, including how and when to use them, what they do, and how they do it. The purpose of detailing these tools is to showcase them as part of a new management theory called human performance management (HPM). HPM provides the foundation for connecting the bottom line to corporations' human potential value (HPV). Some of the benefits of implementing these tools are reduction of turnover, increased customer service, and increased profits and sales. The return-on-investment (ROI) for using the HPM can be as high as 1,000 percent.

What Does Human Performance Have to Do With Business? Nothing?

Early in my consulting career, an assessment of a call center demonstrated to me how systemic and prevalent is the practice of not valuing people as a business asset. Members of the assessment team and the author evaluated the call center, determining its *"as is"* and *"could be"* states, and made a business proposal for change. While part of the team's change proposals were focused on technology, process, organizational structures, resources, capital, and the like, none of the team members had considered people as a strategic part of the plan. In my proposal, I suggested the connection of people to the bottom line in a colloquial, but pointed, slogan: "Bad performers, bad business. No people, no business." My teammates intuitively understood what I was saying, but queried me further. I answered, "Do the machines run by themselves? Can the process remember how to follow itself?"

It is clear to me (and to thousands of other people I have interviewed over the past 15 years) that the main ingredient in any business is people because without them businesses cannot run. This is true whether it is a call center or any other business. However, no matter how loudly the phrase *no people, no business* has rung in many of my colleagues' ears, they admit that they do not know how to quantify or measure the value of people to the company. In many cases the measure of the value of human performance has stayed ignored. In addition, decision makers and stakeholders are not sure how to improve the people or human capital aspect of their business.

In interviews I had with managers over the years, they have said without hesitation that the most time-consuming and difficult aspect of their job was dealing with people issues. Whether the issue was the day-to-day motivation and management of people, training people on new technology, setting up new teams, implementing change, or resolving conflict, managers dreaded the work, saying it took an extraordinary amount of time they wanted or needed to spend on other things. Even when they did spend time on the people part of business, they were not able to get the kind of performance or behavior changes they really needed to make the business successful. I began asking them, "What is the cost of dealing with people and the return-on-investment?" and I found they did not have an answer, though most felt dealing with people had some effect. The unanswered questions are: How do we

- fight and win the war for talent? (recruiting)
- invest in and receive a return on intellectual capital? (training)
- evaluate employees to create a true learning environment and increase the intellectual capital? (evaluating)
- create real value that could be seen on a profit-and-loss (P&L) sheet? (ROI for HPM).

Training Example: Training to Increase Conflict Resolution Skills Capabilities

To properly set the stage for the value of the upcoming tools, I wanted to provide a real-life example of how training, for instance, could have a great impact on the business. This example looks at the ROI for training a manager to have more efficient and effective conflict resolution skills when dealing with her employees.

The formula for calculating ROI is:

$$ROI = \frac{\text{Net program benefits}}{\text{Program costs}}$$

This example spotlights two managers, Stacey and Kevin. Stacey has a poor relationship with her employees and spends approximately six hours per day in conflict with them. She needs management training. Kevin has better management skills and spends only about two hours per day resolving people issues in his department. Both earn $50 per hour, approximately $100,000 per year.

The first thing to look at are productivity calculations, which show where the two employees' time and energy are being spent. A productivity calculation for Stacey tells upper management that she has only two productive hours out of eight, and the company is not getting the most out of her. The calculation for Kevin, who spends most of his day doing productive work (six out of eight hours), shows that he is 75 percent productive.

Following are the productivity calculations for Stacey and Kevin:

Stacey: 2/8 hours $= .25 \times 100 = 25\%$ productive
Kevin: 6/8 hours $= .75 \times 100 = 75\%$ productive

It is more impressive is to look at the next level of measurement, which compares the cost of a training solution as corrective action with the cost to the company of Stacey's lack of management skill. Since Stacey is always dealing with people issues, she is only productive 25 percent of the time. The following calculations show that Stacey is earning $75,000 to be in conflict with her employees.
- Productive Work
  — Stacey: $.25 \times \$100,000 = \$25,000$
  — Kevin: $.75 \times \$100,000 = \$75,000$
- Being in Conflict
  — Stacey: $.75 \times \$100,000 = \$75,000$
  — Kevin: $.25 \times \$100,000 = \$25,000$

The impact of the cost hits home if you ask yourself, What if that salary were coming out of my wallet?

Now consider the cost of a training solution. An average management training course can be estimated to cost about $2,000 for a day. Often that training day can include other managers, so the return can be even higher. In this case we will just look at the impact of changing Stacey's management skills.

The benefit of the solution is an 80 percent improvement in Stacy's time dealing with conflicts. An 80 percent improvement in a $75,000 cost of conflict amounts to $60,000, as the equation shows:

$$.8 \times \$75,000 = \$60,000$$

The cost of the solution is the cost of the day of training, which is estimated at $2,000. To calculate the ROI, you subtract the cost of the solution from the benefit of the solution, divide that amount by the cost of the solution, and multiply that answer by 100, as follows:

$$ROI = \frac{\text{Benefit of solution} - \text{cost of solution}}{\text{Cost of solution}} \times 100$$

$$ROI = \frac{\$60,000 - \$2,000}{\$2,000} \times 100$$

$$ROI = \frac{\$58,000}{\$2,000} \times 100 =$$

$$ROI = 29 \times 100$$

$$ROI = 2,900\%$$

The ROI is 2,900 percent, so the cost of training Stacey is well worth the investment.

With this kind of simple yet direct calculation, executives and managers can clearly see the value of using the tools available to increase their organization's human performance.

Theories Transformed Into Tools

Business has traditionally measured the bottom line in one of two ways: the quantity of gross profits or the quantity of net profit. New measurement systems to measure the true value are becoming recognized. As little as one-third to one-half of most companies' stock market value is accounted for these days by hard assets, such as property, plant, and equipment. The lion's share of measurement should lie in intellectual property, or what has been coined soft skills or invisible assets. This author would like the business world to regard as assets such items as customer satisfaction, internal business processes, an organization's ability to learn and grow, and the effectiveness of the corporate culture, and to erase the notion that these have no effect on the bottom line. Although they have been excluded from itemization on an accounting sheet because they are deemed not to affect the bottom line, they have a real effect and value. I would like to challenge the accounting community to reformulate the financial accounting model to incorporate the valuation of the company's invisible assets. The Financial Accounting Standards Board has recently formed a committee to study this. Placing values on these "invisibles," the HPV, requires an entirely new set of accounting tools.

Part of the reason the financial reporting process has not shifted is that it is anchored to an accounting principle developed centuries ago. The process today is highly standardized and governed by a set of generally accepted accounting principles, or GAAP, which are widely recognized by lenders, investors, regulators, and others. GAAP standards tell companies how and when to deduct expenses in the current fiscal year or to amortize them over several years. They describe how to assign other costs such as legal, consulting, and overhead to each widget coming off an assembly line. The key in this current system is objectivity, exactness, and comparability. Inherent in financial accounting is the language of traditional business—concrete, pragmatic, and measurable.

Attrition Calculation Tool

Data is the price to the boardroom. My experience at a high-tech company illustrates what I mean. I had to hire 100 people in six weeks. This was a tall order to fill because it was summer, when many people are on vacation; the company had had many layoffs; it had a high turnover rate; and it had lost its reputation as an employer of choice. The ratio of interviews to hiring in this field was about one to 10. Hiring 100 people meant interviewing about 1,000.

I took two steps. I created an innovative recruiting program, and I began looking for a root cause for the company's attrition. The question I asked myself and others was, "We could hire more people, but why was our retention so low?" When I asked management if we were concerned about the time and money spent on re-recruiting people, its response was, "People come and they go." However, my intuition said that turnover translated into dollars, but I did not have the data to back that up.

Information from *Inc.*/Gallup surveys (1996-2000) and from our own focus groups revealed that retention could be increased if employees felt they
- were part of a learning organization
- were given the opportunity to learn new skills (rather than getting laid off)

- were challenged, growing, and expanding
- had a manager who cared about them (their development and well-being)
- were rewarded for their work, especially after downsizing and the doubling of workloads
- were treated with respect.

Figure 1 illustrates the responses from our employee focus group. The logical conclusion was that our HPM model needing changing—everything from how and whom we were recruiting and hiring to new hire training, employee development, evaluation, and ultimately retention. We needed a new model for cultivating the human potential asset.

Feeling very confident that I had identified the corrective actions needed to solve the root cause of the problem, I asked top-level management for $6 million for an HPM program that would focus on recruiting, training, employee development, and evaluation. This company, like most, scoffed at adding people to its debt-asset sheet.

Discouraged, but forging forward, I set out to find the data to show the value of a program to increase the human potential and value of the company. I collected information from several respected colleagues and managers, asking them to estimate the cost of replacing an engineer who had been there five years. While it was a rough calculation, everyone came up with similar figures: $150,000 per employee. I compared this figure with Jack Phillip's (1997) turnover costs analysis (as shown in table 1), and found it to be right on.

I took no action for two months, during which time 40 people left the company. At the next company meeting, my presentation read:

$$\$150,000 \times 40 = \$6 \text{ million}$$

Top-level management asked, "What is that about?" I said, "You know that six million I asked for? It was spent on attrition." There was silence in the room. I followed with, "And you know in the last year, 200 people left. You do the math." And I ended with, "Even if my numbers are off by 50 percent, that's still a lot of money to be spending on attrition. You wouldn't knowingly waste money like that on anything else, would you?" They quickly responded, "So what exactly did you want that money for?" I had gotten their attention.

That is when I knew data was truly the entry price to the boardroom. The numbers made them instantly interested in what I proposed; the soft skills had just transformed into hard, bottom-line data. When they compared the $6 million needed for an HPM program with

Figure 1. Why good employees leave a company.

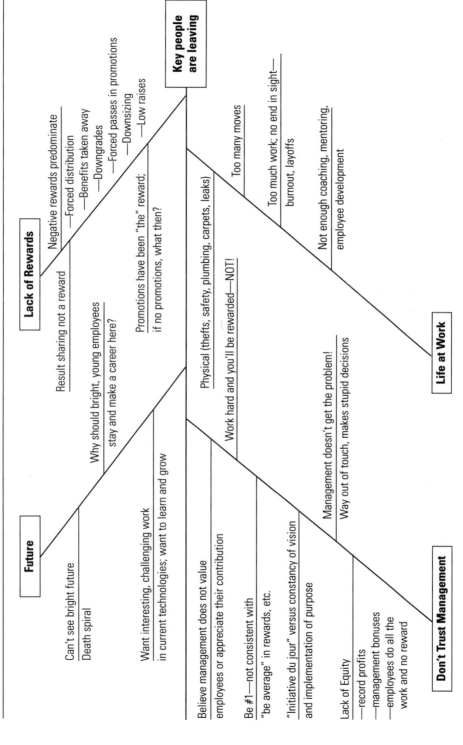

Key people are leaving

Future

Can't see bright future
Death spiral

Why should bright, young employees
stay and make a career here?

Want interesting, challenging work
in current technologies; want to learn and grow

Lack of Rewards

Negative rewards predominate
—Forced distribution
—Benefits taken away
—Downgrades
—Forced passes in promotions
—Downsizing
—Low raises

Result sharing not a reward

Promotions have been "the" reward;
if no promotions, what then?

Believe management does not value
employees or appreciate their contribution

Be #1—not consistent with
"be average" in rewards, etc.

"Initiative du jour" versus constancy of vision
and implementation of purpose

Lack of Equity
—record profits
—management bonuses
—employees do all the
work and no reward

Physical (thefts, safety, plumbing, carpets, leaks)

Work hard and you'll be rewarded—NOT!

Too many moves

Too much work; no end in sight—
burnout, layoffs

Not enough coaching, mentoring,
employee development

Management doesn't get the problem!
Way out of touch, makes stupid decisions

Life at Work

Don't Trust Management

Table 1. Turnover costs summary.

Job Type and Category	Turnover Cost Ranges as a Percent of Annual Wage and Salary
Entry level—hourly, nonskilled (e.g., fast food worker)	30-50%
Service/production workers—hourly (e.g., courier)	40-70%
Skilled hourly (e.g., machinist)	75-100%
Clerical/administrative (e.g., scheduler)	50-80%
Professional (e.g., sales representative, nurse, accountant)	75-125%
Technical (e.g., computer technician)	100-150%
Engineers (e.g., chemical engineer)	200-300%
Specialists (e.g., computer software designer)	200-400%
Supervisors/team leaders (e.g., section supervisor)	100-150%
Middle managers (e.g., department manager)	125-200%

Notes:
1. Percents are rounded to reflect the general range of costs from studies.
2. Costs are fully loaded to include all of the costs of replacing an employee and bringing him or her to the level of productivity and efficiency of the former employee. The turnover included in studies is usually unexpected and unwanted. The following costs categories are usually included:
   - exit cost of previous employee
   - lost productivity
   - recruiting cost
   - quality problems
   - employee cost
   - customer dissatisfaction
   - orientation cost
   - loss of expertise and knowledge
   - training cost
   - supervisor's time for turnover
   - wages and salaries while training
   - temporary replacement costs.
3. Turnover costs are usually calculated when excessive turnover is an issue and turnover costs are high. The actual cost of turnover for a specific job in an organization may vary considerably. The above ranges are intended to reflect what has been generally reported in the literature when turnover costs are analyzed.

Sources of Data
The sources of data for these studies follow three general categories:
1. Industry and trade magazines have reported the cost of turnover for a specific job within an industry.
2. Publications in general management (academic and practitioner), human resources management, human resources development training, and performance improvement often reflect ROI cost studies because of the importance of turnover to senior managers and human resources managers.
3. Independent studies have been conducted by organizations and not reported in the literature. Some of these studies have been provided privately to Performance Resources Organization. In addition, Performance Resources Organization has conducted several turnover cost studies, and these results are included in this analysis.

the $30 million they were spending on attrition a year, they realized that they had to pay attention to my request.

Until the paradigm shifts completely in the corporate setting, the importance of people to the bottom line may need dramatic demonstrations.

Human Performance Value Tool

While many decision makers might recognize that intellectual capital does matter, the challenge lies in figuring out what it is and how to increase it. David Ulrich (1999) provides a formula:

$$\text{Intellectual capital} = \text{competence} \times \text{commitment}$$

To make this theoretical model practical, I suggest assigning values to each of these so that an HPV can be calculated to give a quick rough assessment of what the overall value is of the human potential. Then it is possible to determine what needs to be changed in your group or department in the areas of recruiting, training, or evaluating.

Take a quick assessment of all the employees within in your sphere of influence, rating them for commitment and competence. To assess your department or group, ask yourself:
• What category do your employees fall into?
• What category would you like them to be in?

For instance, give a grade on a five-point scale to competence and commitment, such as:
• high competence = 10
• low competence = 5
• high commitment = 10
• low commitment = 5.

If the five employees in table 2 were both committed and competent, then the HPV for this group would have a score of 500. Some of the employees are lacking in either competence or commitment, however, so the score is lower. The result is that the HPV is at 60 percent of what it could be, as the following equation shows. If you are paying someone a dollar, for example, and the person is only doing work that is worth 60 cents, you are losing money.

$$\text{Actual/Potential} \times 100 = \text{Percentage of Total HP Value}$$
$$300/500 \times 100 = 60\%$$

Table 2. Assessment of HPV.

Employee Name	Competence	Commitment	HPV Actual	HPV Potential
Susie	10	10	100	100
Charlie	5	5	25	100
Fred	10	5	50	100
Jane	5	5	25	100
Joey	10	10	100	100
HPV Total			**300**	**500**

The goal is to get each employee to strive toward a mark on the HPV scale of approximately 100 percent. Table 3 illustrates the range of values for four employees with a mix of high and low competence and commitment. A company's aim should be to have a competent and committed employee. Companies in which there is high competence but low employee commitment may have talented employees who cannot get things done. In comparison, a company might have very committed employees, who are not as smart as their competitors and make wrong decisions or do dumb things. Both types of employees are dangerous. Companies should assess the HPV at the individual level unit and then for the whole firm. This type of exercise gives management a concrete way to begin to understand the need for improvements in the HPV and in their performance management systems.

The competence part of this model can include items like customer loyalty, productivity, profitability, and prediction of business outcomes. The closer the measure of the actual performance is to the

Table 3. HPV rating criteria.

	High Competence	Low Competence
High Employee Commitment	Keeper—star 10 × 10 = 100	Provide training to improve 10 × 5 = 50
Low Employee Commitment	Give feedback; if no improvement, fire at your convenience 10 × 5 = 50	Fire today 5 × 5 = 25

measure of the potential, the better the business outcome will be. Individual employees can be measured with respect to increases in knowledge, skill, and their commitment to set and reach goals within the scope of the project, on time, and within budget. Personal assessments can then be accumulated into a collective assessment of the intellectual capital within a unit. The chapter on performance evaluations by Tanya Koons and Jonetta Pettway gives examples of performance management forms and suggestions on very specific measurement criteria for competence.

James Brain Quinn (1999) defines professional intellect as
- cognitive knowledge
- advanced skills
- systems understanding
- self-motivated creativity.

The challenge for managers is to develop and leverage this intellect. Firms with the ability to secure intellectual capital will be more productive, and they will be better able to change in this competitive marketplace, meet customer expectations, and beat their competition.

Goal Setting to Manage Human Performance

HPM is the effort to improve the individual and collective performance in an organization. HPM includes methods, tools, and processes that realize opportunities and redirect, correct, motivate, and maintain performance. HPM is most effective when it is applied at all levels in the organization: to executives, managers, individuals, business units, and the whole organization. This type of application requires that a people strategy be part of the strategic planning and that decision makers begin to embrace people as part of their assets. Following are some of the most sophisticated tools, examples, and scientific methods of enhancing HPM.

Start by Aligning Business Goals With Individual Goals

Human performance management systems can be designed to obtain tangible results measured by improvements in sales, productivity, quality, morale, turnover, safety records, profits, and ROI. The first step is to align employee goals and learning with corporate strategy. Every measurement project needs to begin and end with a clear connection to the business results. Companies often set strategic goals, but do not communicate them in a way that makes clear to the employees what they are supposed to do on a daily basis to reach those goals. In addition, employees are not always measured directly against their own goals. Many times the performance evaluation system is not set up to track what an employee does on a day-to-day basis with tangible results like increases in sales and productivity.

Without understanding a company's sequential flow of goals and their connection to a measurement system, employees are left on their own to fill their days with the work they think they should do. Most employees are well intentioned and come to work to do a good job. However, without taking the time to communicate, educate, and agree on how corporate goals map into business unit goals and then into individual goals, companies leave employees to create their own priorities. These priorities can be based on whatever the employees deem important: those things they like to do or are good at or that have the most political correctness. These priorities do not necessarily have the best interest of the company in mind.

Figure 2 shows a clear flow of goals from the corporate level to the individual level. The difference between enhanced productivity and busy work is reviewing everything and making a plan, that is, mapping the corporate goals to the goals of the division, department, teams, and individuals.

Figure 3 shows the interrelatedness of goals within a department. When working with companies, I have found that people are very busy; they are answering emails, returning calls, writing reports, and so forth.

Figure 2. Goal flow.

But when I ask what goals these activities map into and what business outcome the people want to reach as a result of the effort, they respond with a blank stare. It is not that the people do not want to answer, but that they are spending so much time fighting fires or doing things that are not really important that "they are not focusing on the things that matter most," as Stephen Covey (1990) said. Again, this is not the employees' fault, but that of the culture. The culture must allow people to spend time on planning and goal setting so that employees can prioritize and manage their activities in concert with business results.

Contracting for Alignment on the Goals

The goals can be any number of things, such as to increase sales or expand innovation, each of which requires employees to take different actions. Once the people at the top decide the goals, it is necessary to convey the message throughout the company. Depending on the corporate makeup, the heads of the smaller units within the company—whether a department, business unit, or team, for example—must tell their staffs both the corporate goals and those of their area. With those two sets of goals, managers and their individual employees can contract to do the work to obtain the results. Figure 4 depicts an employee-manager contracting session.

Figure 3. Direct correlations of department goals with individual goals.

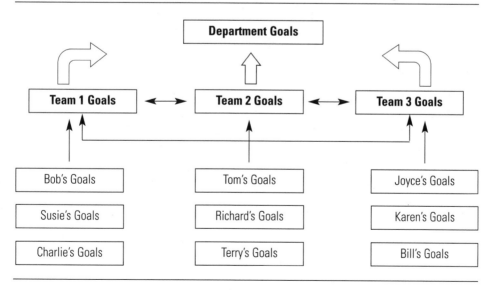

Figure 4. Employee-manager contracting session.

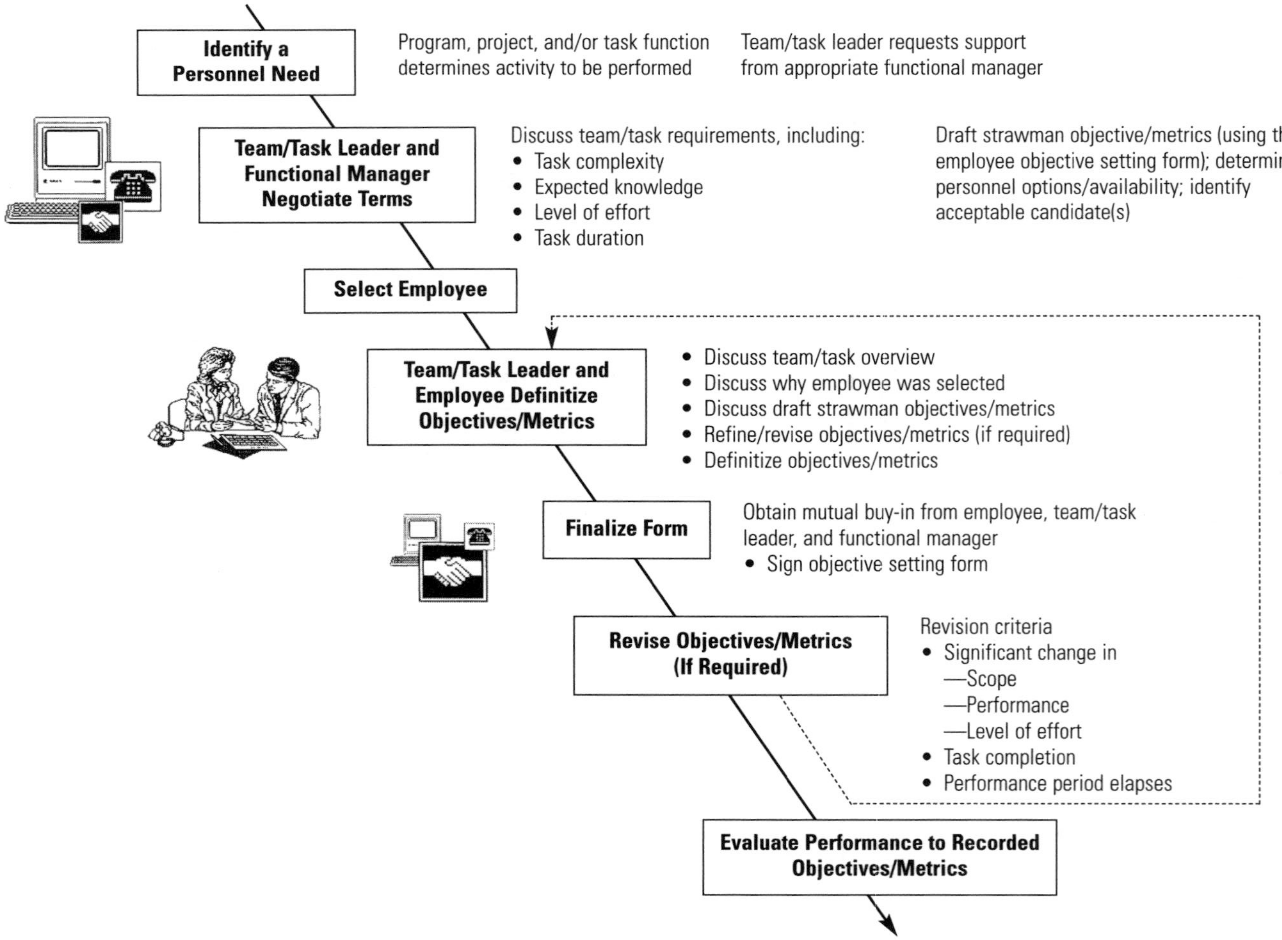

Identify a Personnel Need

Program, project, and/or task function determines activity to be performed

Team/Task Leader and Functional Manager Negotiate Terms

Team/task leader requests support from appropriate functional manager

Discuss team/task requirements, including:
- Task complexity
- Expected knowledge
- Level of effort
- Task duration

Draft strawman objective/metrics (using the employee objective setting form); determine personnel options/availability; identify acceptable candidate(s)

Select Employee

Team/Task Leader and Employee Definitize Objectives/Metrics

- Discuss team/task overview
- Discuss why employee was selected
- Discuss draft strawman objectives/metrics
- Refine/revise objectives/metrics (if required)
- Definitize objectives/metrics

Finalize Form

Obtain mutual buy-in from employee, team/task leader, and functional manager
- Sign objective setting form

Revise Objectives/Metrics (If Required)

Revision criteria
- Significant change in
  —Scope
  —Performance
  —Level of effort
- Task completion
- Performance period elapses

Evaluate Performance to Recorded Objectives/Metrics

It is important for managers to spend time with employees to ensure they are working daily toward the right business outcome, but many of them do not have the necessary skills or interest to do that. A change in philosophy may be necessary at some companies to redefine a manager's job from going to meetings and doing paperwork to spending time developing and working with their employees. Some companies may even need to develop a checklist of the skills and attributes needed for these managerial jobs to ensure they choose the kind of people who meet the criteria. Command-and-control type leaders do not fit this criterion, whereas relationship-based leaders do, as described in Judy Rosener's (1997) book, *America's Competitive Secret*.

Recruiting and the Selection and Hiring Process
Background on Winning the War for Talent

According to a McKinsey and Co. study involving 77 companies and almost 6,000 managers and executives (Huselid, 1999), the most important corporate resource over the next 20 years will be talent: smart, sophisticated businesspeople who are technologically literate, globally astute, and operationally agile. And as the demand for talent goes up, the supply will be going down. Companies will have to devise more imaginative hiring practices, and they will also have to work harder to keep their best people.

When assessing your recruiting techniques, ask yourself or your team the following questions to get a handle on where your recruiting philosophy stands in this competitive marketplace:

- How many of you would be interested in a job opportunity that expects you to do the same work, for the same pay, in the same industry, using the same skills, for a long time, without much chance to improve your pay or personal growth?
- How many of you would at least be open to explore an opportunity that is clearly superior to your current situation?

If the Position Could Talk, What Would It Say?

In some fields, it has become an employees' job market. Employees have many choices and when they do not like how they are treated, especially the so-called Generation Xers, they vote with their feet. As described earlier, the cost of attrition is very high. The first step in creating a solid HPM system is to get a tool to help in the selection of competencies. Having used a large range of assessments for over the past 15 years, I have found them to be valuable tools in all areas of HPM. Performance problems often begin as selection issues.

A job competency analysis (JCA) is a tool to match an employee to a company and a job. Chapters 2 (by Anthony J. Adorno and John F. Binning) and 10 (by Jon Anton, Julie Kuliopulos, and Natalie L. Petouhoff) give excellent examples of how this type of selection tool can be used with great results. This kind of process defines and prioritizes the top core competencies required for superior performance. It also allows for a structured selection interview using the questions suggested by a JCA profile and the criteria to produce job descriptions and ads that result in an ideal hire. Excellent sources for all kinds of assessments are www.lmrassociates.com, for LMR Associates, and www.corptools.com, for Corporate Transformation Tools. In addition, training after the hiring of employees is key to employee retention. Important information on the subject appears in the chapters by Trina A. Stephens (chapter 8), Jon Anton (chapter 9), Anne G. Nickerson and Elizabeth A. Ahearn (chapter 11), and Jon Anton and Anne G. Nickerson (chapter 12).

Why a Selection Tool Is Important

Harris Plotkin (1997) states that poor selection methodologies are responsible for many of the performance issues in companies.

- Over 90 percent of all hiring decisions are made by an interview.
- Most selection decision are made in less than an hour.
- A Michigan State University study showed interviewing is only 14 percent accurate in predicting performance.
- HR typically interviews candidates for call center jobs, but HR does not always understand the competencies that are important for a job the way a manager or team leader does.

Selection methodologies are important because turnover costs are on the average 100 percent of an annual salary or more.

Connecting Competency Recruiting to Training to Performance Evaluations

As your organization goes through its yearly strategic planning, it is imperative to evaluate what it takes to perform. One must decide what the competencies are, recruit to them, train to them, and evaluate by them. Although a JCA is a recruiting tool, it is also a tool that provides the most return on the investment when it is used in all aspects of the HPM process.

Measuring Emotional Intelligence

"Employees are hired for their technical resume, but promoted for their emotional (EQ) intelligence," as Daniel Goleman (1998) says.

One indication that EQ needs to be added to the HPM models is the success of Daniel Goleman's book *Emotional Intelligence.* Goleman has shown that EQ competencies are twice as important today as technical competencies. EQ competencies relate to abilities like self-control, self-awareness, and empathy. He has shown that developing these competencies requires a different learning process than developing technical competencies. Various methods for teaching EQ appear in the following case studies in this book: Koons and Pettway; Engdahl and Perdue; Voellinger; McLafferty; and Lavoie. In addition, a JCA is another tool to enhance the EQ in your organization and the HPV.

The Gap Between Workers and Companies

JCA is accurate because it is based on current research into people's behaviors and attitudes. The old way of recruiting, training, and evaluating will not work because the workforce has dramatically changed. Managers who do not understand this do not have the right people with the right commitment or competencies.

In the short history of the working world, a remarkable shift has occurred in the relationship between the workplace and the employee. There has been a greater understanding of cause and effect, and that has resulted in many theories on behavior change. The shift took place, in part, because of the influence in the field of human potential from the works of Freud and Jung and other scholars of psychology and psychiatry. An offshoot of the scholarly theory and traditional therapy is the field of self-help.

As the human performance movement has gained momentum via a more conscious collective mindset, people like Deepak Chopra, Andrew Weil, and Carolyn Mess have propagated the self-help field with books on their experiences and ideas on personal change. Everyone from psychologists to physicists has solutions to change human behavior.

In the same timeframe, the evolution of personal consciousness among many other things created a gap in the satisfaction of workers in jobs. While workers were getting enlightened via self-help, corporations were still operating under command-and-control leadership originating from the military and followed management practices and processes pioneered by Fredrick Taylor (1998) in his *The Principles of Scientific Management* and William Whyte's (1956) *The Organization Man.*

With today's strong economy, attrition is high and expensive so becoming an employer of choice is among a company's largest challenges. Via employee exit surveys, employers are finding that keeping workers with fast knowledge acquisition, skills, and attributes greatly depends on how they are treated by management, their work-life balance, and the working environment.

Because of businesses' need to re-create culture and improve technology and processes, change management was born. It and its associated billion dollar businesses have flourished via professional services companies and consulting firms. However, of the $80 billion of corporate change programs, 85 percent of CEOs report that the changes were not effective. The objectives and results projected were not realized through the current methodologies applied. Most of this has to do with the concentrated focus of these change programs on technology and workflow process and little or no attention given to the human potential aspect of the change process. At the end of the day, if people do not change, process cannot remember how to follow itself and technology cannot turn itself on. It still comes down to the people.

Using a JCA Tool for Selection
The principle feature of a JCA is its comprehensive, computerized process for collecting and analyzing multiple inputs to define and prioritize core competencies for performance. The primary benefits are efficiency, cost-effectiveness, and objectivity. The competencies are made of skills, behaviors, attitudes, knowledge, beliefs, and intelligence. These include the following:
- teamwork
- conflict management
- interpersonal skills
- problem solving and decision making
- creativity and innovation
- customer service
- leadership and management
- employee development and coaching
- written communication
- flexibility
- goal setting
- political adeptness
- personal effectiveness
- presenting skills
- negotiating
- persuasion
- empathy

- continuous learning
- futuristic thinking.

A JCA is an evaluation tool that detects the core competencies for a job. The typical process begins with a one-hour brainstorming session in which candidates discuss the position, and the discussion is followed by filling out a position survey. The survey enumerates and ranks the required competencies. The information gained can then be transferred and reused in the interviewing, training, and evaluation processes. A client, a newly transferred creative director at a large communication company, used the tool to help determine if transferring someone at the company from one job and department to another would be a good fit. This newly transferred creative director felt it was a very useful process in helping the employee assess herself for this move to a sales position.

The products of a JCA are a detailed list of core competencies and an example of what that behavior looks like. Because they are so complete and detailed, the descriptions make it easy to write job advertisements and job descriptions. Along with the core competencies is a set of behavioral interview questions that directly applies to assessing candidates' capabilities with respect to those core competencies. Following is an example of a JCA for customer service:

CORE COMPETENCY: CUSTOMER SERVICE. Customer service is defined as anticipating, meeting or exceeding (or both) customer needs, wants, and expectations.

Top customer service competencies descriptions:
- strives to anticipate, identify, and understand customers' wants and needs and concerns
- responds to customers with a sense of urgency
- follows through on customer requests
- is patient and courteous with customers
- resolves issues and complaints to the satisfaction of customers
- expends extraordinary effort to satisfy customers
- develops relationship with customers
- partners with customers to assist them in achieving their objectives
- acts as an advocate for customers' needs
- takes professional risks for the sake of the customers' needs.

BEHAVIORAL INTERVIEWING TOOL FROM A JCA. The interviewer, who has given a candidate a JCA, wants to hear how the potential service representative would make an extraordinary effort to respond to the customers' needs and wants to be certain the candidate speaks to customers' in a way that would ensure satisfaction. The interviewer should probe for as many details and specifics as possible, such as names, dates, and other verifiable information as well as for the candidate's thoughts or feelings about a situation.

Following are some examples of behavioral interviewing questions:
- Describe a situation where you were given outstanding customer service. What made that stand out?
- Give me an example of a situation in which you improved the level of customer service in your organization. What did you do to improve it? What was the outcome?
- Give an example of when you were given special recognition or acknowledgement for going the extra mile to satisfy a customer.
- Describe a situation in which you took a stand for a customer.
- Describe the most difficult customer you've ever had to deal with and how you handled the person.
- Describe a situation in which you felt a particularly demanding customer might have been trying to take advantage of you or the organization.

Multirater 360 Feedback Evaluation and Employee Development Tool

In addition to the core competencies, a JCA can provide a panoramic picture of performance via a multirater 360 survey. This tool is useful when employees need to know how they are perceived by their peers, superiors, and direct reports. Employees are surrounded by this information daily, but it tends to stay hidden or unspoken and sometimes is distorted. By gathering the data from everyone in the employee's work circle, a complete picture of an individual's skills is produced. This picture reveals strengths to build on and specific areas of performance improvement. A computerized system is more objective than the traditional method in which the manager is the only evaluator, and it evens out personal favoritism. A multirater feedback tool also makes the data collection and analysis very practical.

Assessments can be customized for a number of uses including leadership, customer service, teamwork, and supervision. If a technical person is moving into a merchandising position, for example, the employee's supervisors may undertake a multirater 360 feedback survey to get a baseline of the employee's skills and to develop the individual's self-awareness as a manager.

All aspects of the survey would be on the computer, including the assessments. The associates who answer the survey questions would reply to the questions on the computer. The replies to the survey questions would generate a report, which the employee under review would get by keying in a code. The associates' feedback would also reveal the kind of help the employee needs, and those needs would generate a workbook to help the employee develop the necessary skills.

The employee can share the report with the raters so they can stay involved to help the person reviewed to grow. Employees find this process invaluable because they have a clear picture of their abilities and how to improve on them. This kind of internal and personal buy-in is one of the most important aspects of changing work-related behavior. By giving employees a tool to improve as well as to have the support of the people around them, they are able to develop, gain a higher degree of alignment with their goals, increase their commitment and competency, and open up the discussion of improving the HPV of the company and themselves.

Training Process
Background on Tool's Importance

Promoting learning to make something happen in the business differently requires that the training objectives be tied to business outcomes. This of course requires that the trainers know and understand the business outcomes. Because they need that information, HRD and training professionals need to be part of the strategic planning team along with CEOs, chief operating officers, chief financial offers, and others in and outside of the company. Without this detailed, inside information, training to raise the HPV cannot occur. This flow of information can be enhanced via a goal flow-down process, like that shown in figure 3. When corporate goals are communicated and department and individual goals are defined and clear, training can be designed to obtain the business outcomes and measured against those outcomes.

Behavioral Work Talents and Values Tools

One of the most helpful training tools to increase the HPV is a behavioral work talents and values (BWTV) tool. This kind of tool helps employees be more of who they already are, both professionally and personally. Employees become clear about who they are, making them more effective and productive employees and people. In addition, it helps make phenomenal changes in workers' interactions with bosses and co-workers and with managing up, laterally, and down. Many assessment tools of this type are available to companies, as described at the Website www.lmrassociates.com.

Two consultants for the Gallup Organization (Buckingham and Coffman, 1999) detail the degree to which behavioral talents are the key to organizational success. The data is based on in-depth interviews of over 80,000 managers in over 400 companies. The findings show that those managers and colleagues who focused on turning each employee's behavioral talents into performance had the greatest productivity, job satisfaction, and retention.

To transform these ideas into action, employees and managers need how-to tools. Assessments and the training that goes with them are key to the how-to transformation work behavior. In giving the assessments, it is important that people do not feel that they are being tested, but rather that the purpose is to understand how unique their talents are. There are no better answers or a way to score better. Each person needs to see himself or herself as special and perfect. The ability of people to see their value is the ability to which they can see the value of others. And their ability to appreciate others increases the HPV of the company.

The Value of the Two Assessments

The combination of the behavioral work style analysis and values assessments helps employees to increase their emotional intelligence by enabling them to analyze both the behavior they bring to the job and the behavior required to be successful in that job and on a team. This increase in emotional intelligence serves them the rest of their career and life. Companies create their own language and culture around the assessments, increasing their everyday use and effectiveness.

Managers and employees may benefit from understanding the profile by
- taking control of their decisions and life
- increasing the value of life, satisfaction, and fulfillment
- developing an increased appreciation for the uniqueness of others
- understanding the causes of conflict in communicating with others
- enhancing communication with others so they are understood
- enhancing communication with others so they are able to understand them
- reducing misunderstandings and conflicts
- increasing the enjoyment of working in a team.

The Behavioral Work Style Assessment

The behavioral work style analysis provides information on one's behavioral talents for handling decisions, interacting with people, handling pace (change), and viewing procedures (rules). Many of these assessments are based on the DISC behavior model. That model, which groups behavioral responses into one of four categories—dominance, influence, steadiness, and conscientiousness—has been in existence in various forms since Hippocrates in 400 BC. William Marston took it forward in 1928 with *The Emotions of Normal People.* When employees are aware of those behavioral styles and talents, they have the power and knowledge to modify their behavior for a maximum effect. One's behavioral talents can be adapted to others via:

- tone of voice
- pace of speaking
- the words used
- body language.

Behavior: What We Do

Common examples of behavior are how people:

- show up in a meeting or a conversation
- solve a problem
- interact with others.

The assessment profile can contain information like:

- general characteristics about work style and behavioral talents
- value to the organization
- a checklist for communicating with the person
- things people should not do when they communicate
- ways to improve communication skills with others
- the person's ideal work environment and keys for others to motivate the person
- an action planning page for goal setting and performance management for improvement.

Theory of the Behavioral Work Style Analysis

Each person, through the nature-nurture process, develops a unique behavioral design. This behavioral design is one's window of communication. If a person interacts with you according to your behavioral design, you will tend to open the window of communication. If a person intentionally or unintentionally interacts with you against your behavioral design, you will tend to partially close, completely close, or lock the window of communication.

Personal Values Assessment

Consciously or unconsciously, every decision or course of action is based on our experiences, beliefs, attitudes, and values. For example, the willingness to make tough decisions or take the time to achieve a difficult goal is based on what people feel is valuable. Values direct our actions and offer stimuli for behavior. Values provide the initiative for the diligent pursuit of a goal or vision. As we learn what truly motivates us, we will have far greater insight into why our work is satisfying, why we are top performers, and why we are thriving.

Values represent the why behind what we do. For example, if an employee is participating in a discussion, activity, or career that is in line with that person's attitudes, he or she will find value in that experience. But if that discussion, activity, or career is not in line with the employee's values, the person may react indifferently or even negatively and feel stress, boredom, frustration, or the like.

This profile from the behavioral work style analysis helps the manager to understand the whys behind an employee's actions:
- What is it that causes them to move to action?
- What are the drivers of their behavior?
- What activities, careers, and conversations inspire their passions?

The Power of Communication Training

Ask yourself, "Why it is important to learn how you influence people or solve challenges?" The research at LMR Associates in human behavior found over the last 20 years that:
- Power is the ability to create a desired effect.
- Creating desired effects is performance.
- Performance is maximized when communication is clear.

Conversations in organizations are not just to achieve understanding or agreement on an intellectual level. They are to be in union, both intellectually and emotionally, to accomplish a specific set of actions. Enhanced communication skills allow employees to focus on a core skill set of interpersonal skills to help them reach their individual and team goals. Effectiveness can be improved by having the skills to move others from initial indifference to moderate interest to the full, whole-hearted commitment to move to action.

Conclusion

Human performance management is a system for increasing the HPV. Increasing the HVP increases business outcomes such as sales, productivity, and retention. When a company focuses its recruiting, training, and evaluation processes on business outcomes, it increases not only the HPV, but also the value of the company.

References

Buckingham, Markus, and Curt Coffman. (1999). *First Break All the Rules.* New York: Simon & Schuster.

Covey, Stephen. (1990). *Seven Habits of Highly Effective People.* New York: Simon & Schuster.

Goleman, Daniel. (1998). *Emotional Intelligence and Working With Emotional Intelligence.* New York: Bantam Books.

Huselid, Mark A. (1999). "Impact of Human Resources Management Practices on Turnover, Productivity, and Corporate Financial Performance." *AMA Journal,* 63, 3.

"The *Inc.*/Gallup Survey." (1996-2000, June). *Inc.*

Marston, William. (1928). *The Emotions of Normal People.* New York: Harcourt Brace.

Phillips, Jack J. (1997). *Measuring Return on Investment* (volume 2). Alexandria, VA: ASTD.

Plotkin, Harris. (1997). *Building a Winning Team.* New York: Griffin.

Quinn, James Brain. (1999). "Managing Professional Intellect." In *Delivering Results,* David Ulrich, editor. Boston: Harvard Business Review Press, p. 253.

Rosener, Judy. (1997). *America's Competitive Secret: Women Managers.* New York: Oxford University Press.

Taylor, Fredrick. (1998). *The Principles of Scientific Management.* New York: Dover. (Originally published 1911.)

Ulrich, David, editor. (1999). *Delivering Results.* Boston: Harvard Business Review Press.

Whyte, William H., Jr. (1956). *The Organization Man.* New York: Simon & Schuster.

Suggested Readings

Fitz-enz, Jac, and Jack J. Phillips. (1998). *A New Vision for Human Resources.* New York: Crisp Publications.

"Gallup Organization: New Research Links Emotional Intelligence with Profitability." (December 1998). *The Inner Edge Journal,* 5.

Hodges, Toni Krucky. (1999). *Measuring Learning and Performance.* Alexandria, VA: ASTD.

Holton, Elwood F., III. (1995). *Conducting Needs Assessments.* Alexandria, VA: ASTD.

"Measuring the Invisibles." (March-April 1999). *Business Spirit Journal,* 1.

Petouhoff, Natalie L., Lisa M. Schwartz, and Lana Ruffins. (June 2001). "The Importance of Managing the Human Aspects of Projects:

Costs, Schedules and Performance Risk Management Tools." White Paper Presented at Women in Technology Conference.

Phillips, Jack J. (1991). *Handbook of Training Evaluation and Measurement Methods*. Alexandria, VA, ASTD.

Phillips, Jack J. (1994). *Measuring Return on Investment* (volume 1). Alexandria, VA: ASTD.

Phillips, Jack J. (1997). *Return on Investment in Training and Performance Improvement*. Alexandria, VA, ASTD.

Phillips, Jack J. (1998). *Implementing Evaluation Systems and Process*. Alexandria, VA: ASTD.

Rosener, Judy. (November-December 1990). "Ways Women Lead." *Harvard Business Review*.

Employment Testing to Reduce Call Center Employee Turnover

Health-Care Corporation

Anthony J. Adorno and John F. Binning

Many call centers face the uphill battle of trying to keep call center agents in their seats long enough to break even on their training investment. To reduce employee turnover, call centers need a staffing solution to predict employee fit and retention. In this case, a major U.S.-based corporation in the health-care industry and a consulting firm that specializes in employee turnover reduction teamed to determine the effectiveness of a staffing test for increasing retention.

Independent of this case study the consulting firm, through intensive job analysis and test development efforts, created the Call Center Fit Index (CCFI). The CCFI is an employment test that is standardized, yet tailored specifically for the call center industry.

This case study describes the implementation of the CCFI for this client and its effectiveness for identifying those applicants who are most likely to remain employed.

Organizational Profile
Description of the Center, Customers, and Technology

This health-care corporation owns and manages many domestic and international hospitals. The call center division operates two centers that together act as an extension of a hospital's billing office and are responsible for health-care payment collection services. Both call centers are internally based, and total approximately 700 employees.

This case was prepared to serve as a basis for discussion rather than to illustrate either effective or ineffective administrative and management practices. Names of places, organizations, or people have been disguised at the request of the author or organization.

The data in this case study was gathered from the smaller of the two centers. This center is based in the Southwest, employs roughly 260 people, and houses 175 call center agent seats.

Among the 260 staff members employed in this center, there is one chief operating officer (COO), two directors, 12 managers responsible for between 20 and 30 employees each, and 12 team leaders. Agents at this facility handle a blend of both inbound and outbound contacts. All agents are fully empowered, so there is no formal escalation or second-tier process. In the event that agents need assistance from a team leader, the transition is an informal one in which the team leader may quickly resolve the issue directly with the agent or simply take over the call.

The call volume is approximately 200,000 per month. The average time to close a case ranges from 55 to 65 days. The center currently uses fax, call recording, and automated dialer technology, and it plans to expand to email and online payment options in 2001.

Recruitment, Training, and Evaluation Process

Both full- and part-time call center agents are recruited through the local newspaper. The job primarily attracts high school graduates because the only qualification is prior customer service experience. The leniency of the existing selection system is a major contributing factor for the center's annual turnover rate, which was initially approximately 116 percent. The annual turnover rate was decreased to 100 percent as a result of increased base pay rates and improvements in the center's career pathing system.

The call center environment is relaxed, but with a goal-centered focus. Agent training is focused on enhancing general customer service, account handling, and system skills. The well-rounded training curriculum is delivered through a 10-day program that includes demonstrations, role-playing, and on-the-job instruction. Both operations management and professional trainers developed the program. Agents learn about handling customer issues through educational videos and additional role-playing, which integrates actual customer account information. The greatest challenge for training new call center agents is ensuring mastery of the computer systems and programs, which are unique to the client organization and can be difficult to learn.

Agents are evaluated using numerous performance metrics including collections resolved, number of different accounts worked, amount of productive time, and the like. They are kept informed of the call center's goals for maximizing performance through a variety of team meetings and memos as well as real-time goal reviews on the system. The center utilizes cash bonuses to motivate agents to meet performance goals and offers to retrain employees who fail to meet the center's goals. The center uses a progressive disciplinary system to motivate agents when their failure to achieve performance goals is not a result of deficits in their training.

Understanding Call Center Employee Turnover

All employee turnover is classified into two general types: involuntary and voluntary. Typically involuntary turnover includes dismissals, layoffs, and forced retirement. Because labor market conditions largely affect involuntary turnover rates, they obviously are difficult to manage directly. Fortunately this call center, like most, is not as greatly affected by involuntary turnover as it is by voluntary turnover.

Causes for voluntary employee turnover (such as high stress, unpleasant physical or interpersonal working conditions, monotony, and poor direct supervision) can be managed. Call center agents do not quit because they lack the skills or abilities to perform the job; they quit largely because they are not interested and challenged by the job, lack the personality characteristics to be successful, or are dissatisfied with the environment in which they work. This analysis is supported by decades of professional research which indicates that in addition to such other factors as pay and benefits people report the "opportunity to perform interesting work" as a highly important determinant of job satisfaction. Research also indicates that job satisfaction is one of the best predictors of employee turnover. In other words, employees who report being the most dissatisfied with their work also are the ones who are most likely to quit.

Using this logic, one methodology for reducing call center agent turnover is to identify applicants during the recruitment process whose interest and personality characteristics are consistent with those associated with longer tenure on the job. When there is a good fit, or match, between the applicant and the job, there is likely to be less absenteeism and tardiness and increased employee retention. When there is a poor fit between the applicant and the job, the applicant is not likely to stay in the job for very long, which means his or her employment had a negative impact on the organization because of its investment in orientation and training.

The Call Center Fit Index

The Call Center Fit Index (CCFI) is a standardized, 20-minute preemployment test administered either via paper and pencil or the Internet. It is a combination of both job-specific interest and personality assessment. The test is based specifically on determining the person-job fit.

Procedurally, job applicants respond to a series of items in two sections on the CCFI. In the first section, there are 40 questions, which are designed to assess a job applicant's level of tolerance for performing the job duties of a call center agent. A special questioning format is used to prevent applicants from answering in a manner that is socially desirable, but inconsistent with their true feelings. Purposely selecting the most socially desirable answers to questions is technically referred to as *impression management* and is a problem that reduces the validity and reliability of many personnel selection tests. An example of an item from the first section of the CCFI follows. Applicants must select two statements among each set of four that they find to be the most personally frustrating or aggravating:

a. Being rejected by others.

b. Being evaluated according to closely monitored statistics.

c. Working with dissatisfied customers or clients.

d. Working under conditions that may be physically uncomfortable.

In the second section, applicants respond to a series of 70 statements indicating the degree to which they are personally descriptive. When combined strategically, these represent the most researched and supported model of normal personality assessment called the Big Five, or the five-factor model. Applicants select a one-to-five response for each item, the descriptors for which range from "seldom" to "often." Sample items follow:

1. I am a relaxed, easygoing person.

2. I enjoy bending the rules.

3. I remain calm in a crisis.

4. I get tired of doing things the same old way.

When information from the two sections is combined, the result is a profile of the applicant's level of job "fit," which is described in terms of a *turnover risk rating*. There are three possible turnover risk ratings that an applicant can receive: high turnover risk, marginal turnover risk, or low turnover risk.

Costs and Administration

The consulting group and its client, the health-care corporation, shared the costs of administering the CCFI. The data collected from the study allowed both organizations to conduct validation research on the CCFI. As a result of this mutually beneficial arrangement, the total direct cost to the client was only $1,000. This fee served to defray the costs incurred by the consulting firm for data entry, scoring, reporting of test results, and preparing a summary of the results following completion of the project. The client agreed to collect CCFI data from close to 400 applicants for call center agent positions between each of its two centers.

At the time of the project, the Web-based platform for administering the CCFI was not available, so all data was collected with the more traditional paper-and-pencil version. Typical costs for implementation of the CCFI would be slightly more costly than those reported earlier. Costs vary according to the mode of administration (paper or Web) and the type of test reports selected by the client organization. Fees can range from $8 to $18 per applicant before volume discounts are considered. Thus, if this were a standard implementation for a client using the CCFI administratively for making employment decisions, costs for testing 400 applicants could range from $3,200 to $7,200. At the time of this publication, there were no annual or licensing fees for the CCFI.

The CCFI was administered to a sample of applicants. Seventy-two of them were subsequently hired for entry-level call center agent positions. All applicants were asked to complete the CCFI and were not told in advance of its research nature. The purpose of the test was not disclosed to applicants to ensure that it was completed with the same level of effort as if it was actually being used administratively.

Once the client organization decided whom to hire, the consulting firm gave it very basic information about the test results, such as the applicants' social security numbers (for tracking purposes), their overall test scores, and a turnover risk rating. The information was to enable the client to independently verify any subsequent analyses and results the consulting firm delivered following the project.

Results

Among the 72 applicants who were hired were a total of 32 Caucasians, 19 African Americans, 13 Hispanics, seven Asians, and one American Indian. There were 17 male and 55 female applicants in the group, of whom some took full-time and some took part-time positions.

Predictor Data

All applicants received one of the three turnover risk ratings based on their CCFI profiles. For the sample of 72 total applicants, 25 were rated as high risks, 24 as marginal risks, and 23 as low risks.

Ratings for the high- and low-risk groups have concrete, identifiable implications for employment decisions. That is, it is recommended that high-risk applicants not be given further consideration for employment, and that low-risk applicants continue through the hiring process. For the marginal-risk group, however, it is difficult to predict the likelihood of their turnover. Therefore, the following analyses will primarily consider the effectiveness of the CCFI for correctly identifying the turnover likelihood for both the high- and low-risk groups. Since an incorrect low-risk rating imposes a much greater expense on the organization than an incorrect high-risk rating, it is critical that great accuracy be achieved for the low-risk group.

Turnover Data

To determine the effectiveness of the CCFI for identifying relevant turnover risk groups, the consulting firm collected turnover data six months from the onset of the project. At the time of data collection, all agents had the opportunity to have at least a two-month tenure. The data included start and end dates of employment as well as a classification for the turnover reason (that is, quit or fired). Table 1 shows the number and percent of agents in each turnover category.

Data Analysis

The CCFI was effective for correctly identifying low-risk applicants, and somewhat effective for identifying high-risk applicants.

The consulting firm rated 25 applicants as high risk, and 13 (52 percent) of these agents quit by the time turnover data was collected. Conversely, of the 23 agents rated as low risk, only five (22 percent) quit. The bar chart in figure 1 depicts the findings for the low-risk group with the percentage employed on the vertical axis.

The marginal-risk category was split fairly evenly. One interesting finding for this group was the difference in employment status of full-time and part-time agents. Of the 16 part-time agents rated as

Table 1. Employment status of agents.

	Frequency	Percent
Quit	28	38.9
Fired	1	1.4
Working	43	59.7
Total	72	100

Figure 1. Employment status of the low-risk group.

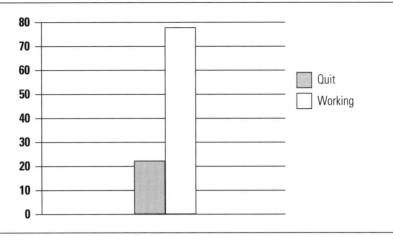

marginal risk, only six were still employed. However, seven of the eight full-time agents who were rated as marginal risk were still employed. While this pattern of results is interesting, more data must be analyzed before firm conclusions can be made about the difference.

The accuracy of the CCFI is confirmed with the type of correlation analysis commonly used to demonstrate the predictive validity of selection systems. Scores on the CCFI correlate significantly with voluntary turnover ($r = .24*$, $p < .05$, uncorrected). This correlation demonstrates that people who score well on the CCFI are likely to remain employed.

Estimating Turnover Reduction

MODEL ONE: ELIMINATING THE HIGH-RISK APPLICANTS. The call center's turnover rate was approximately 40 percent (29 divided by 72) from November 1999 to March 2000 for people hired following completion of the CCFI. If the CCFI had been used administratively during this time, turnover could have been reduced to approximately 29 percent if all high-risk applicants had been screened out of the hiring process. This equals a 28 percent reduction in turnover.

The low-risk rating was accurate 78 percent (18 divided by 23) of the time. If the 25 high-risk applicants were screened out and replaced with low-risk applicants, approximately 20 agents (25 times .78) would still be employed, and five would have quit or been fired. Table 2 shows what a revised table might look like.

Table 2. Potential employment status of agents.

	Quit	Working	Total
Marginal	11	13	24
Low Risk	10	38	48
Total	21	51	72

The revised turnover rate for this same period could have been 29 percent (21 divided by 72). To calculate the reduction in turnover divide 29 (the new turnover rate) by 40 (the old turnover rate) and subtract that figure from 1, as shown:

$$29/40 = .725$$
$$1.0 - .725 = .275 \ (28\%, \text{ when rounded})$$

MODEL TWO: ELIMINATING THE HIGH- AND MARGINAL-RISK APPLICANTS. If the client organization were to have screened out the 49 high- and marginal-risk applicants and hired 49 applicants who received low-risk ratings, approximately 38 (78 percent) would likely still be employed. Table 3 shows what a revised table might look like.

By hiring only those applicants who received low-risk ratings, the company could have had a level of turnover of 22 percent (16 divided by 72) instead of the observed six-month turnover rate of 40 percent. If the client had selected only low-risk applicants, its turnover could have been reduced by 45 percent, as these calculations show:

$$22 \text{ (the new turnover rate)} / 40 \text{ (the old turnover rate)} = .55$$
$$1 - .55 = .45$$

Figure 2 shows the turnover rate for the six-month period, and figure 3 shows the reduction in turnover during that period.

Table 3. Potential employment status of agents.

	Quit	Working	Total
Rating: Low Risk	16	56	72

Figure 2. Turnover rates for the six-month case study period.

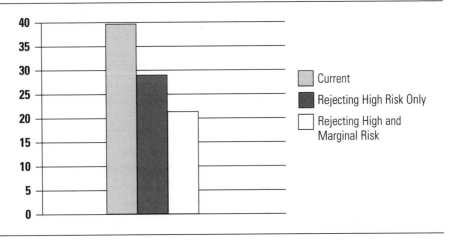

Figure 3. Percent reduction in turnover for the six-month case study period.

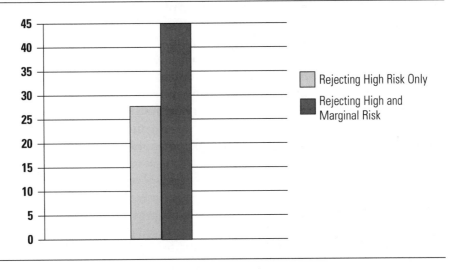

Estimating Cost Savings

MODEL ONE: ELIMINATING HIGH-RISK APPLICANTS ONLY. The client, in communications with the consulting firm, made a conservative estimate that $4,000 was invested per agent in recruiting, testing, and training. Given these estimates, the CCFI could have saved over $28,000 (less testing costs) under the assumptions of model one.

To arrive at this figure, find the current number of total agents who have quit (28) and subtract the estimated number of quits if the CCFI had been used administratively (21). Multiplying seven fewer people times $4,000 gives $28,000 in savings.

Depending on the level of detail requested in CCFI test reports, costs can range from $8 to $18 per applicant. For testing 72 applicants, the client company could have invested between $576 and $1,296. Therefore the net return-on-investment using model one ranged from $26,704 to $27,424 over a six-month period.

MODEL TWO: ELIMINATING BOTH HIGH- AND MARGINAL-RISK APPLICANTS. Estimated savings realized by the client organization using this selection model could approximate $48,000. To arrive at this figure, find the current number of total employees who have quit (28) and subtract the estimated number of quits if the CCFI had been used administratively (16). Multiplying 12 fewer people times $4,000 equals $48,000 in savings.

Again, this figure would be reduced by the amount invested in CCFI testing. Selecting only low-risk applicants could have yielded a net return-on-investment ranging from $46,704 to $47,424.

Since the savings calculated as a result of reduced employee turnover was for a six-month period, savings can be annualized fairly easily. While data has not been collected to reflect the following figures, they are calculated assuming that the same rate of turnover reduction is attained. Therefore, for a one-year period, this client could have saved close to $56,000 under the assumptions of model one and $85,000 under the assumptions of model two.

Summary

Steps can be taken by call center executives to make their operations more profitable and their customers more satisfied, by reducing employee turnover. The type of turnover that plagues call centers is voluntary turnover. Voluntary turnover results from a lack of fit or congruence between the interests and personality characteristics of call center agents and the interests and personality characteristics required for the job. Many hiring managers may lack the resources necessary to help make this determination, which will often result in poor fit or match between the agent and the job. This misfit creates a costly and inconvenient problem, but a manageable one.

This case study presents strong empirical evidence supporting the power of the CCFI for reducing voluntary turnover in a call center. The design of the study permitted a controlled analysis of each turnover risk group since the client organization made all employment decisions without the aid of the CCFI test results. These results support the validity and cost-effectiveness of the CCFI.

Executives can use the theoretical model presented in this case study for assembling their own selection system designed to reduce voluntary employee turnover. With a thorough understanding of the underlying causes of employee turnover, practitioners can integrate both interest and personality assessment into their existing staffing systems in a strategic manner to select only the best job applicants. Selecting or developing similar personnel selection instruments should be performed very carefully and only by trained professionals with an expert knowledge of personnel selection and validation issues. Unfortunately, practitioners desiring to use or develop other tools would have to conduct extensive research in order to determine how best to use such instruments in order to produce the best turnover prediction model. Obviously this also would greatly increase the cost for implementation, but the long-term return-on-investment could be almost as great.

Regardless of the route selected, if you are a call center executive or practitioner, start to take action. Use professional research as a competitive advantage and value your employee recruitment and selection systems as much as your training program, realizing that it has a profound effect on your entire call center operation. After all, where is the value in extensively training someone if the person will not stay with your company?

Questions for Discussion

1. What are the underlying reasons for employee turnover in call centers?
2. How is the CCFI designed to predict turnover likelihood for job applicants?
3. Why was the method of implementation used by the client organization advantageous to studying the effects of the CCFI?
4. How do you calculate the percentage of turnover reduction using an existing turnover rate?
5. How do you analyze the return-on-investment for using an intervention like the CCFI?
6. Why is it important for organizations to participate in professional research?
7. What is most consistently reported as the most important determinant of job satisfaction?

8. What is a common problem of many personnel selection systems that result in reduced validity and reliability?

9. What factors would lead an applicant to receive a rating of marginal risk on the CCFI?

10. In your opinion, why would an incorrect rating of low risk on the CCFI impose a greater cost to the organization than an incorrect rating of high risk?

The Authors

Anthony J. Adorno is vice president of the DeGarmo Group, a management and HR consulting firm based in Bloomington, Illinois. Adorno received his master's degree in industrial and organizational psychology from Illinois State University. He has spent several years researching employee turnover in call centers and has served as an invited speaker at both regional and national conferences. He helped to develop the Call Center Fit Index, and has co-authored book chapters and articles that have appeared in both professional and trade publications. He specializes in personnel selection and validation issues, and serves as an editorial advisor for two call center trade publications. He can be reached at the DeGarmo Group, Inc., 305 Woodland Avenue, Bloomington, IL 61701; phone: 309.438-1435; fax: 309.820.1715; email: adorno@degarmogroup.com.

John F. Binning is president of the DeGarmo Group. He received his M.A. and Ph.D. degrees from the University of Akron. Binning is on the faculty at Illinois State University where he is an associate professor of industrial and organizational psychology. His research has been published in *Journal of Applied Psychology, Academy of Management Journal, Organizational Behavior and Human Performance,* and *Human Resource Management Journal.* He regularly provides editorial reviews for a variety of professional journals. For more than 15 years he has consulted with organizational clients on projects such as selection system design and validation, EEO compliance, performance appraisal, training design and implementation, as well as managerial assessment and succession planning.

Suggested Readings

Adorno, A.J. (July 2000). "Understanding and Combating Call Center Employee Turnover." *Customer Contact World Magazine,* 26-31.

Adorno, A.J., and J.F. Binning. (1999). *Call Center Fit Index (CCFI) Validation Report.* Bloomington, IL: DeGarmo Group.

Adorno, A.J., and J.F. Binning. (1999). *Analysis of Employee Turnover and Job Performance for Call Center Representatives.* Bloomington, IL: DeGarmo Group.

Adorno, A.J., and J.F. Binning. (October 6-7, 1999). "The Call Center Fit Index: An Innovative Approach for Cost-Effective Turnover Reduction. *Call Center Manager's Report.* October, 6-7.

Binning, J.F., A.J. Adorno. (December 1998). "The Job Congruence System: A System for Reducing Turnover." *IPMA News: The Newsletter of the International Personnel Management Association,* 24-25.

Binning, J.F., J.M. LeBreton, and A.J. Adorno. (1999). "Personality Assessment." In *The Employment Interview Handbook,* R.W. Eder and M.M. Harris, editors. Thousand Oaks, CA: Sage.

Binning, J.F., J.M. LeBreton, and A.J. Adorno. (April 1999). *The Role of Personality Assessment in the Employment Interview.* Paper presented at the Annual Conference of the Society for Industrial and Organizational Psychology, Atlanta, GA.

Binning, J.F. and G.V. Barrett. (1989). "Validity of Personnel Decisions: A Conceptual Analysis of the Inferential and Evidential Bases." *Journal of Applied Psychology, 74,* 478-494.

Performance Evaluations: A Practical Guide and Examples for Call Center Employees

Edcor

Tanya Koons and Jonetta Pettway

This case study is a practical approach to performance feedback. Most of its examples can be used as a template for use in call center environments. By applying the performance evaluations the authors describe in this chapter, Edcor has been able to develop an internal culture that builds teamwork and overall employee job satisfaction. It has also supported the ability to maintain longevity of key personnel through a hands-on approach to building their skills and development. Edcor has experienced explosive growth and understands the need to develop and nurture employees to take on that next level of expertise to support the growing needs of the business. This development process is a win-win situation for Edcor and the personnel it supports.

This case study details the performance feedback tool designed to keep communication flowing, build employees' skill sets, and determine standard operating expectations and guidelines to ensure high-quality services. It also describes the tool's value in retaining employees who are already fully functional in their positions.

Company Background

Since the 1980s, Edcor has been an industry leader in providing integrated technology and single-source, outsourced services for corporate education and training, tuition assistance, and customer relationship management solutions. The company offers one of the only completely integrated approaches—from consulting to fully operational functionality—

This case was prepared to serve as a basis for discussion rather than to illustrate effective or ineffective administrative and management practices.

and provides advanced technology, full-service capabilities, and high-quality standards.

Edcor has over 400 employees, including more than 200 contact center agents, over 40 systems and programming professionals, 55 client relationship managers, and executive and administrative staff. Most employees are located at the Edcor headquarters, in Pontiac, Michigan, and the remaining staff resides on-site at client facilities throughout the United States and abroad.

With Edcor as its single-source partner, clientele are experiencing the advantages of having a centralized business model, with benefits including increased service levels resulting in consistent program administration throughout all assigned locations, accurate reporting, enhanced response time, and historical record-keeping capable of supporting U.S. government agency requirements such as Occupational Safety and Health Administration and the Food and Drug Administration as well as international trade requirements like ISO 9000. Edcor also provides clients with sophisticated, best-practice targeted recruiting, assessment, training, and retention processes. This centralized business model provides corporate environments with the time and ability to focus on their own core competencies, and to use the resulting information necessary to strategically manage their human capital resources.

Edcor's clientele include such companies as General Motors, DaimlerChrysler, AT&T, Microsoft, Cisco, and UPS.

Hours of Operation

Edcor currently maintains call center support hours from 7 a.m. to 9 p.m. eastern time Monday through Friday to support client-employees in the United States and abroad. The call center conforms to the clients' holiday schedules to ensure that the customer service center is aligned with the service needs of the employees. In addition to the customer service support hours, Edcor operates its computer network 24 hours each day, seven days per week. This around-the-clock operation allows the employees and customers to obtain both general and personal account information through integrated voice response (IVR) systems and the World Wide Web (www), as well as other multimedia channels, like email.

Technical Environment

Edcor uses state-of-the-art technologies to deliver its services, and this requires a dedicated and focused training and performance management system to make sure its employees are able to leverage the technology to best service their client base.

Numerous clients endorse Edcor's use of email as a viable means of communication with their employees. They also use the Web to disseminate and collect information. Many clients are using the company's IVR solutions to collect test scores and process enrollments as well as Edcor's extensive fax-server and scanning capabilities.

Edcor tailors its solutions to meet its clients' business, technology, and security needs. For example, Edcor can support point-to-point connectivity, SSL encryption over the public Internet, IP-based rules to restrict and inhibit access, and ANX connectivity or VPN technology as dictated by an organization's security and technology policies and capabilities.

Advanced technology is not limited to the data side as the telephone-switching platform represents one of the most advanced call center solutions currently available. Automatic call distribution (ACD) software enables advanced queuing and call-routing functions. Computer telephony integration (CTI) and IVR systems integrate with the telephone switch to provide a coordinated, cohesive solution to Edcor's clients. Call monitoring capabilities are deployed on desktops throughout the facilities as well as on callboards placed in the call center. This technology provides the ability to access detailed, continuously updated statistics on individual agents, telephone calls, queue times, agent availability, and the like.

Edcor's solutions are supported by a clustered Web farm, which leverages multiple servers for the Web services as well as application processing. Distributed databases are utilized to eliminate contention and congestion at the database level. The solution is built on Intel-based WinNT/2000 architecture. SQL Server 7.0 is used as the database engine with the application level supported using Microsoft's ASP and COM architecture.

An Aspect switch is used to support the call center environment. The switch provides the ability to define client-specific call routing, overflow and after-hours routing, and extensive monitoring and reporting of call center activity. The Edify voice response system is used to support self-service and after-hours processing.

Edcor continually invests in the acquisition and implementation of new technologies and researches other technologies. As each of the technological changes is made, the training and performance management system is updated to educate and measure performance.

Employee Development and Evaluation Methodology

It is important to create a methodology for evaluations that is based on the employee demographics and company culture. In this case study, we, the authors, share the ideas behind our practices to help the readers understand our methodology and take those ideas and integrate them into their own cultures. Evaluators in most companies dread the whole process of evaluations, in part because it is time-consuming and may involve co-workers' sensitivities. The process requires leaders to spend time assessing their performance (output) against the company's performance standards by using measurable descriptions and examples whenever possible. Especially difficult are those cases where critical feedback is needed to change a behavior or improve a much-needed skill set. The goal is to offer feedback and make specific suggestions for change in such a way that the evaluation promotes a behavior or mindset change and does not discourage or upset the individual. The approach the evaluator takes should support positive changes and not cause the evaluatee to walk away disappointed in the review of his or her performance.

An understanding of the issues evaluators struggle with makes it is easier to design an evaluation process, forms, and procedures that help overcome their fears and develop their ability to feel good about doing evaluations. This chapter describes our methodology and specific tools. It is advisable to develop a full package with tools because it simplifies and speeds implementation, provides consistency, and makes it easy to manage with little or no involvement from HR.

Writing the Evaluation

The two basic ingredients for writing an evaluation are knowledge of the person to be evaluated and knowledge of how to write an evaluation. First, an evaluator should be sure he or she knows about the person. It is important to review the person's entire contributions and performance for the period being evaluated. In Edcor's environment, we use performance logs to track positive accomplishments, learning experiences, and areas that a person has struggled with. By keeping this record as a working document, an evaluator can easily recall all the events, dates, and examples with a quick review of the log. Second, it is important that the evaluator be familiar with the evaluation form, the standards, and rankings. One of the most difficult parts of the process for many evaluators is translating their knowledge of the employee into appropriate language on the form. The goal is to have an evaluation that will be most helpful to the person being evaluated, so the language must be clear, honest, and unambiguous.

This chapter provides a variety of tools to help evaluators convey their assessment to the employees in the most useful way. The tools are as follows:

- a list of suggested words to fit each rating category
- sample competency skill descriptions
- a list of adjectives and verbs to describe performance
- a list of phrases to describe key skills
- sample review forms.

The listings of words and phrases are helpful tools for jumpstarting the thought process. They also provide both experienced and first-time evaluators with the same cultural vocabulary so that there is consistency across the company. For first-time evaluators, a template of phrases helps them focus on the specific feedback they want to communicate.

Edcor uses these tools in its evaluation training course and finds it helps develop skills for both the evaluator and evaluatee. The authors recommend that organizations give their staff an evaluation-training refresher course just before evaluation time each year.

Setting the Tone

The written assessment is only one part of the process. How an evaluator presents the evaluation is just as important as what he or she says in it. Because the written assessment and presentation are so closely entwined, it is necessary for the evaluator to first describe the process so the employee can better understand the guidelines the evaluator followed and his or her conclusions. The process and the guidelines include things like reviewing the evaluation scale and defining each rating and the standards that support each category. Evaluations are confidential, so each evaluator should meet in a private setting with the employee who is under review. Edcor evaluates staff according to the following scale:

- needs improvement
- meets expectations
- exceeds expectations.

The company wants to clearly communicate to the employees that a "meets" means good or very good performance. An employee who does not understand that terminology could feel he or she is just ordinary or adequate. Here is an example of how to set the tone for the review.

Jayne, overall your review this year was very positive. You have really developed your skills in many areas. There are also some areas where I want to continue to develop your skills too. I thought it was important to recognize all your major contributions as well as some areas to work on for future development, and I think this review fairly represents that. I would like you to review my comments and then let's take some time to talk about my feedback and your goals moving forward.

This way the stage is set so the employee feels the feedback is overall very positive, but she is not alarmed when she sees the "needs improvement" box checked. People by nature see the check marks before they see the words behind it. If the evaluatee has negative first impressions, it would be hard to turn that around and have a meaningful and nondefensive discussion. It helps to set the tone first. The following is an example of setting the tone for a review that is not as positive as Jayne's:

John, I want to take some time to give you feedback on your progress this year. Overall I feel positive about the progress you made, but you will find several comments about areas in which you are still struggling. I want you to recognize what the main themes are and offer you specific suggestions about how to continue to make progress in the areas in which "needs improvement" was marked. I want you to know that with a little coaching and a development plan, I see you becoming more established within the team.

An evaluation is not the appropriate place to reprimand an employee or write up a disciplinary action form, even if the employee is getting critical feedback, as John was. The feedback should provide the evaluator with an opportunity to drive the employee toward a change in behavior or in a skill set. It can be determined later and in another format if an employee's issues are so severe that the person should start down the disciplinary process. If you are presenting a "write up," usually the situation and feedback has already occurred but the employee has not or does not take the feedback and incorporate it into his or her work environment.

Similarly, an evaluation is not the appropriate situation in which to offer promotions. In many companies, evaluation, development, and promotion are all part of the same process. The employee development process at Edcor is separate from the promotion process.

The company does not promote someone because of the time of year, but rather when that person has developed the skills and experience needed to take on the new role. Once the person has have obtained the appropriate skills and experience, he or she now has the opportunity to apply or be considered for a new role if one becomes available. The evaluation process helps identify areas to work on to allow time for that skill to be developed, so the person can be ready for the next available opportunity when it arises.

The wording in an evaluation should reflect the philosophy that promotions are separate from reviews. For example, Edcor does not name or promise a position when writing a review because doing so could put the company in a compromising situation. The person involved could, for example, never accomplish the skills, but might point back to the review as a commitment to put him or her in that role. In addition, if a company focuses on a skill set instead of a title, an employee has an opportunity to develop for more than one future position. The following examples illustrate the difference between naming a role or skill set and naming a specific title or position.

> In the future, I see you taking on a leadership role within the team, after you've had some coaching and encouragement and have gained a better understanding of the Web solution process.

Compare that language with the following example that promises too much:

> For future development, I see you becoming a team leader.

If an employee has false expectations about his or her performance or about the likelihood of receiving a raise or promotion, we always ask ourselves the following questions:
- Is it management's fault?
- Did we give appropriate feedback during the year to assist the employee in being successful to meet his or her job objectives?
- Were we able to be honest about the employee's performance?
- Did we give concrete examples of what was good or excellent and what would be better if the employee took another action?
- Was there even a future open opportunity for that position? Has the business needs of the organization changed so much over time that now the company has eliminated or reduced the number of open positions for that title?

We feel it is more valuable to focus on developing a skill set that might lead the employee to the next position than it is to name an actual position.

Performance Evaluation Timelines

Planning is the most important step in giving evaluations. Evaluations need to be incorporated into the leader's regular roles and responsibilities. It works best to give evaluations to employees as they are completed, rather than to wait until all of them are done. Figure 1 is a calendar that helps evaluators to visualize and plan for the evaluations. A calendar like this can help an evaluator integrate the process into an already busy month. We publish the schedule to all Edcor personnel, finding that helps with accountability for both the evaluators and the employees being evaluated. Table 1 shows the general process of the evaluation in each phase and describes key points.

Putting the Review on Paper

Both style and substance are important to a performance review. It is important to begin with a rough draft. The evaluator can rework it as often as necessary so that the final copy says only what will be helpful to the person being evaluated. Figure 2 is an example of an evaluation form for call center agents and senior agents. Figure 3 is an excerpt of the comparable form for team leaders. The excerpt displays only the information that differs from that in the agents' sample review form. Both are ready to be completed.

It is also important to keep the file for the person under review close at hand. It will be necessary to consult it for specific examples to substantiate the comments.

An employee's most-recent performance is likely to be fresh in mind, but a review is for a year's worth of work. If Suzy was below standard all year, but in the last 30 days she has made a great deal of progress, the evaluator would have to take that into account. The evaluation has to be on the whole year's progress, not just the last 30 days. The evaluator must justify the rating by acknowledging the change in behavior, saying something like, "Although you have recently made progress in improving your phone skills in the last 30 days, you need to continue to focus on your ability to tactfully convey information to employees."

Allow sufficient time for the process. Employees deserve a well-thought-out review so they can learn how to do the best job possible.

Figure 1. Scheduling evaluations.

November

Sunday	Monday	Tuesday	Wednesday	Thursday	Friday	Saturday
			1	2	3	4
5	6	7	8 Write Reviews through 22nd	9	10	11
12	13	14	15	16	17	18
19	20	21	22	23 Written Reviews Completed	24	25
26	27 Reviews Given	28	29	30 All Staff Reviews Should Be Given		

Table 1. Timeline and guidelines for performance evaluations.

If hired after September 1	Complete 60-day evaluation
Hired before September 1	Complete annual evaluation
Transferred departments within the last 60 days	Current management team owns evaluation process. Consult with previous management team for input.
Prereview worksheet (annual review only)	Employee completes prior to receiving evaluation. Follow up with staff to remind of due date but do not put off completion of the evaluation based on receipt of prereview worksheet.
Remain objective	Utilize materials and tools used to document performance and behavior. Refrain from using personal opinions, *stick to facts. Don't evaluate on just the last quarter performance. Look at performance for the full year.*
Final copy of evaluation	Can be handwritten or on line typed as long as the final on line version is deleted once a physical copy is printed. DO NOT save evaluations online.
Routing of the final copy of the evaluation	All signed documentation needs to be forwarded to the proper management staff and ultimately be placed in employee's permanent personnel file. Duplicate records should not be kept at any level. It is not necessary to keep duplicate records. If appropriate you can view an employee's file and what it contains.
Multiple positions	When writing an evaluation, factor in the time in which the employee has held his or her current position. Employees may have held different positions within the last year. If you're evaluating a team leader who has been in that role for two months, for example, factor that in your scoring and comments.

It takes time and care to assess a year's performance and to say things in the most helpful way.

Style

Following are tips on an appropriate style for written evaluations:

- Begin with a rough draft that can be edited and proofread.
- For neatness and appearance, use either a pen or pencil, not both on the final review.
- Do not cross out mistakes. Instead, start over. Limit the use of correction fluid to cover mistakes. Otherwise, you'll have to find a way to explain why you changed "meets standards" to "needs improvement."

Figure 2. Sample review form for agents.

Performance Evaluation   _____60 Day   _____Annual

Employee Name: _____   Date: _____

Team: _____   Position: ESR/SESR Agents

Hire Date: _____

I.   **Areas of Evaluation:**
Basic Skills
SESR Feedback

II. **List the specific functions and/or skill sets the employee should focus on for future growth and development:**

III. **Performance Definitions:**

- **Exceeds Expectations:**
Results consistently exceeded basic job expectation in that area. Recognition is warranted due to higher than expected productivity and special contributions.
- **Meets Expectations:**
Results were fully acceptable and satisfactory.
For those employees in their position less than one year: Results indicate that employee is making acceptable progress toward fully acceptable performance.
- **Needs Improvement:**
Results were minimally acceptable and satisfactory overall, but certain areas of performance require improvement before employee is fully at an acceptable performance level.

Upon Completion of Review:
Required signatures in the following order:
1. Employee
2. And/or supervisor depending on team structure
3. And/or manager depending on team structure
4. And/or general manager depending on team structure
5. Director
6. VP
7. CEO
8. Personnel file

(continued on page 52)

- Be consistent. Use upper and lower case or all upper case for a professional look.
- Consult with your management team when needed. Do not be afraid to ask for assistance, guidance, or direction.
- Performance reviews are confidential, so conduct discussions with employees about their performance reviews in a private setting.

Figure 2. Sample review form for agents (continued).

Area of Evaluation (Place a check in the box that most fits the area of evaluation)

Customer Service Skills/Communication	Needs Improvement	Meets Expectations	Exceeds Expectations
The ability to effectively listen to and properly respond to service inquires and to communicate policy and processes to internal and external customers			

Strengths:

Areas for Improvement:

Telephone Etiquette	Needs Improvement	Meets Expectations	Exceeds Expectations
Consistently implements Edcor standards in regard to scripting and observer checklist guidelines			

Strengths:

Areas for Improvement:

Knowledge	Needs Improvement	Meets Expectations	Exceeds Expectations
Maintains an understanding of client(s), position, and Edcor. Utilizes resources such as training tools and manuals for continued training and development			

Strengths:

Areas for Improvement:

Interpersonal Skills	Needs Improvement	Meets Expectations	Exceeds Expectations
Values the contribution of others and open to constructive feedback			

Strengths:

Areas for Improvement:

Quality - Quantity	Needs Improvement	Meets Expectations	Exceeds Expectations
Meets quality and accuracy objectives against set daily output goals			

Strengths:

Areas for Improvement:

Judgment	Needs Improvement	Meets Expectations	Exceeds Expectations
Has the ability to properly identify, analyze, and make reasonable decisions on behalf of the employee, the client, and Edcor			

Strengths:

Areas for Improvement:

Initiative	Needs Improvement	Meets Expectations	Exceeds Expectations
Empowers himself or herself to resolve issues and problem solve. Possesses the ability to actively participate, volunteer, and accept new challenges on his or her own, with minimal direction			

Strengths:

Areas for Improvement:

Technology	Needs Improvement	Meets Expectations	Exceeds Expectations
The ability to integrate technology into the daily work routine. Maintains a basic understanding of company/client technology			

Strengths:

Areas for Improvement:

Team Development	Needs Improvement	Meets Expectations	Exceeds Expectations
Participation in building team morale, unity, and flexibility			

Strengths:

Areas for Improvement:

Attendance	Needs Improvement	Meets Expectations	Exceeds Expectations
Timely and reliable			

Strengths:

Areas for Improvement:

(continued on page 54)

Figure 2. Sample review form for agents (continued).

Area of Evaluation (Place a check in the box that most fits the area of evaluation)

Appearance and Habits	Needs Improvement	Meets Expectations	Exceeds Expectations
Personal habits, clothing, and grooming			

Strengths:

Areas for Improvement:

Adaptability	Needs Improvement	Meets Expectations	Exceeds Expectations
Ability to quickly understand new information, situations, and environment			

Strengths:

Areas for Improvement:

This section should be completed for Senior Positions Only

Area of Evaluation (Place a check in the box that most fits the area of evaluation)

Role Model/Coach	Needs Improvement	Meets Expectations	Exceeds Expectations
Meets the needs of the team, the client, and Edcor for training, assisting with escalated processes and calls. Sets high standards for self and others			

Strengths:

Areas for Improvement:

Job Skill and Responsibility	Needs Improvement	Meets Expectations	Exceeds Expectations
Provides appropriate higher level support in meeting the administrative needs of the team and the client. Meets quality objectives and deadlines of projects and established processes			

Strengths:

Areas for Improvement:

Resource Knowledge	Needs Improvement	Meets Expectations	Exceeds Expectations
Possesses the knowledge to handle the work when team leader is not available. Effective at giving direction			

Strengths:

Areas for Improvement:

Overall Performance Evaluation	Needs Improvement	Meets Expectations	Exceeds Expectations
Please check one (✔)			

Comment on principal strengths:

_____
_____
_____
_____

Areas for improvement on principal weaknesses and suggestions for improvement:

_____
_____
_____
_____

List the specific functions and/or skill sets the employee should focus on for future growth and development:

_____
_____
_____
_____

Employee Comments:

_____
_____
_____
_____

Format

At Edcor, performance evaluation forms have questions that require multiple choice answers and written comments. These comments apply to forms of that type.

- Based on the definition of the evaluation category, rank each statement as exceeds expectations, meets expectations, or needs improvement by placing a check mark in the middle of the line.
- As a general rule, most check marks will be placed in the middle of one of the rankings. If you feel somebody is borderline between ratings, however, mark the line where the employee's behavior best fits.

As figure 4 shows, the person in row A meets expectations about listening effectively. The person in row B does more than meet expectations about listening effectively, but does not quite exceed expectations. When placing a check mark to the far left or right (not directly in the middle) of a ranking, explain why in the comments area.

- Use the comment section to go into detail to fully explain the rating. If you checked the "needs improvement" category, you are required to explain why.
- In written comments, assess the employee's performance in terms of these considerations
  — employee's performance in comparison with department or team standards
  — employee's performance in comparison with individually agreed upon goals
  — positive performance observed or negative performance observed
  — improvement and developmental areas
  — needed or desired training.
- When writing in the comment section, use full sentences, not fragments, to describe exactly what you're saying. Example A is an appropriate explanation that gives Nancy detailed information about her performance. Examples B do not say enough to help the employee.

Example A. Nancy, you have had problems consistently meeting scheduled deadlines and goals in the processing of your daily work.

Example B. Needs to meet goals better
Works well with others

Consistency

Evaluations that are consistent in what they say and how they say it are most helpful to employees. Following are some tips:
- Be sure the performance rating is consistent with your written comments. For example, an evaluator checks exceeds expectations for the Leadership category. However, in the comment section the evaluator writes, "The employee does a very good job at leading the team." There is an inconsistency between the evaluator's comments and the category standard. Although the description "very good" might sound as if the person under evaluation is exceeding expectations, the standards make clear that if someone's performance is good or very good, the appropriate rating would be "meets expectations." It is important to use definitions that are consistent with rankings to avoid inconsistencies among evaluators. In addition, be sure to

Figure 3. Excerpt of a sample review form for team leaders.

Productivity	Needs Improvement (Comments)	Meets Expectations	Exceeds Expectations
Has a thorough understanding of job functions			
Plans and organizes work well			
Utilizes time management skills and tools			
Completes deliverables within the established timeframe; meets deadlines			
Has minimal lates and absences			

Quality Management	Needs Improvement (Comments)	Meets Expectations	Exceeds Expectations
Consistently produces work of high quality			
Provides timely feedback and recommendations for improvement			
Actively provides continuous training of company and team quality practices and tools to include ISO 9002 objectives			
Works with direct report(s) on corrective and preventive solutions for company, client, and team issues			
Monitors training materials and tools and makes timely revisions to ensure client service objectives are maintained			
Keeps accurate and up-to-date employee training records for staff			

Job Knowledge	Needs Improvement (Comments)	Meets Expectations	Exceeds Expectations
Demonstrates a strong, functional knowledge of position, client, and Edcor (conveys accurate client policy information)			
Understands purposes, objectives, practices, and procedures of department/team			
Shares knowledge for the benefit of employees, Edcor, and client(s)			
Possesses the knowledge to handle the work when supervisor is not available			
Demonstrates a working knowledge of all technologies used to process (AS/400, IVR, Web, software applications)			
Empowers himself or herself to offer solutions and participates in coordinating resolution of client and Edcor issues			

(continued on page 58)

Figure 3. Excerpt of a sample review form for team leaders (continued).

Problem-Solving Skills	Needs Improvement (Comments)	Meets Expectations	Exceeds Expectations
Possesses the ability to identify, analyze, and solve client issues			
Actively participates in issue resolution			
Utilizes resources outside of team/department for opinions, insight			
Is able to reach sound conclusions			
Makes timely decisions			

Adaptability	Needs Improvement (Comments)	Meets Expectations	Exceeds Expectations
Adapts well to changing conditions within position, company, and environment			
Maintains constructive behavior under stress			
Is open to new ideas and approaches			
Refrains from overreacting			

Communication	Needs Improvement (Comments)	Meets Expectations	Exceeds Expectations
Is skillful at clearly communicating, both orally and in writing, information and processes with internal and external customers			
Expresses personal and organizational needs in a positive, constructive manner			
Listens and responds professionally after gathering pertinent facts			

Relationship with Others	Needs Improvement (Comments)	Meets Expectations	Exceeds Expectations
Gives constructive feedback in a timely manner			
Builds positive relationships with co-workers and management			
Gains the confidence and trust of others			
Focuses on task or performance rather than personality			
Is sensitive to the needs of staff, employees, and client contacts			
Seeks out and values the contribution of others			

Teamwork (to include working with management and other departments and clients	Needs Improvement (Comments)	Meets Expectations	Exceeds Expectations
Is effective at developing the team to work together to achieve team/company goals			
Is an active, involved participant in team projects and Edcor-sponsored events			
Builds team spirit of working together toward common goals			
Is known to work effectively with others			

Commitment	Needs Improvement (Comments)	Meets Expectations	Exceeds Expectations
Takes pride in work at a personal and team level			
Accepts responsibility for performance of team and self			
Looks for ways to challenge team and self in learning new processes and sharing fresh ideas			

Leadership	Needs Improvement (Comments)	Meets Expectations	Exceeds Expectations
Takes the initiative in identifying and solving problems			
Is effective at motivating employees			
Proposes proactive solutions after objectively thinking through scenarios			
Can implement solutions with little or no direction			
Uses time management skills to consistently meet deadlines			
Leads by example by exhibiting positive professional and behavioral qualities			
Assists in development and implementation of team training objectives			
Is effective at mentoring team on performance and personal issues			

Staff Development	Needs Improvement (Comments)	Meets Expectations	Exceeds Expectations
Uses established training tools and checklists to effectively and efficiently conduct training			
Treats staff and others with respect			
Encourages free and open communications			
Supports and encourages cross-functional training opportunities			
Provides honest, objective feedback on a timely basis			
Is effective at writing and presenting 60-day, 6-month and annual reviews			

Figure 4. Check marks in evaluations.

	Needs Improvement	Meets Expectations	Exceeds Expectations
(A) listens effectively	_____	__X__	_____
(B) listens effectively	_____	__X__	_____

use specific words or examples to back up the ranking, whether it is an exceeds or a meets expectations. The evaluator must also observe and ensure that performance is sustained over a period of time. If an employee was below standard all year, but has shown improvement in the last 30 days, you will want to be sure to mark the appropriate ranking based on the entire year's progress and not just the last 30 days. The following list gives specific words most applicable for each rating category:

— Exceeds Expectations
  • performs with unusual accuracy
  • superior, extraordinary
  • consistently exceeds
  • leader overall, exceeding others and exceeding job requirements
  • people rely on this person's expertise and knowledge on a regular basis
  • outstanding or exceptional performance

— Meets Expectations:
  • produces good or very good quality of work
  • adequate (lower ends of meets)
  • thoroughly understands
  • meets standards or the general guidelines
  • generally understands
  • progressing
  • acceptable performance

— Needs Improvement:
  • substandard performance
  • inconsistent
  • unsatisfactory
  • unacceptable
  • fair performance
  • needs to continue to develop skills in this area
  • slow to make progress, not up to speed, doesn't show initiative.

- Be careful to use time frequency words correctly. "Suzy is always late" is different from "Suzy is sometimes late." Choose the word that best reflects the situation and is consistent with the rating.
  - always
  - sometimes
  - usually
  - occasionally
  - frequently
  - rarely
  - often
  - seldom
  - continuously
  - never.
- Write in a consistent style to avoid any confusion and to give an overall professional look. Write in second person (our preference) or third person but do not flip back and forth. An example of second person is "John, you have done a good job leading the team." Third person would be, "Nancy has done a good job at leading the team."

Clarity

Following are some suggestions to help you convey your message clearly:

- Use significant documentation and factual examples whenever possible. These will help the person under evaluation understand your perspective. Use quantitative or specific examples when expressing your thoughts.
- When determining the goals for future growth and development, make sure to include examples of how to reach these goals so it is clear to the employee what his or her goals are. If the employee needs to improve on his or her phone skills, explain how to do so. An example might be: "Set aside time on a weekly basis to listen to other staff members who provide great service over the phone" or "Provide employees with their own taped calls for review or participate in a peer group tape review." Examples of ineffective statements about future growth and development include:

> Should continue to train and develop her ESR skills

This statement does not say what skills to develop—some of them, all of them, just one of them. Instead, elaborate on the specific skills to work on to achieve the accomplished outcome, which may be to exceed, meet, or promote to the next job level.

Another ineffective statement is as follows:

Ask about upcoming training classes to attend

This statement does not give enough information. If there are 11 courses to choose from, should the employee take all of them? Are there other options than taking a training course, such as job shadowing?

A similarly ineffective statement is

Needs more training going forward

Instead, describe the specific training needed. Be clear and specific when giving feedback. The answer is not always training. It can be coaching, mentoring, or reading further about the industry.

Rate Objectively

You can improve the accuracy of the ratings by recognizing the following factors that subvert evaluations:

- *halo effect:* the tendency of an evaluator to rate a person good or bad on all characteristics based on an experience or knowledge involving only one experience
- *leniency tendency:* a tendency toward evaluating all persons as outstanding and to give inflated ratings rather than true assessments of performance
- *strictness tendency:* the opposite of the leniency tendency; a bias toward rating all persons at the low end of the scale and a tendency to be overly demanding or critical
- *average tendency:* a tendency to evaluate every person as average regardless of major differences in performance.

The way to overcome these traits is to turn personal feelings into objective professional feedback. Stay away from how you feel and state what the situation is. For example,

- Instead of saying, "Jayne, I feel you are . . .," say, "Jayne, you are excellent at coaching and mentoring."
- Instead of, "I think that you may feel . . .," say, "Scott, you often seem intimidated with the process."
- Instead of saying, "I really want to give you . . .," say, "I would like you to take on additional responsibility to help provide you with more challenge on a daily basis."

Sample Competency Skill Descriptions

Edcor uses the following descriptions of competency skills for each category. In Edcor's call center environment, there are multiple levels of call center positions and different expectations at the agent representative, senior representative, and team leaders levels. Where appropriate, the category heading will name which position the competency skill represents. If nothing is specified, that category represents all staff who hold a call center position. Developing these standards assists the evaluator to stay objective and not be swayed by personal opinion. Using the category standard for "adaptability" which follows, the evaluator can quickly determine which ranking an employee falls into based on his or her assessment that the employee has a hard time adapting to the work environment and the team. Again, based on the standard, the evaluator must choose "needs improvement." If an employee disagrees with a particular ranking, the evaluator can point to the standard as a reference at how he or she arrived at that conclusion. The most important aspect of developing the competency standards is that the employee has a clear description of what specifically his or her leader and Edcor expect. The employee knows what it will take to be seen as an employee who "exceeds expectations." This knowledge also helps an employee who falls into the "needs improvement" area. If it is clear in the beginning what behavior or action will lead an evaluator to mark this category, then the employee is likely to accept the feedback.

- Adaptability
  - *Exceeds:* This person has been presented with multiple positions, circumstances or challenging tasks, or both, and has adapted extremely well in all cases. This person has shown great flexibility in adjusting to team changes and taking on different roles within the management team and the organization.
  - *Meets:* This person displays a willingness to work with change in a positive way. This person adapted well to his or her position, integrated successfully as a team member, and adapts to our changing environment. The person is flexible in his or her ability to take on additional responsibility and understands the vision and standards.
  - *Needs improvement:* This person has a hard time adapting to his or her team and the environment. He or she is often coached on a better way to approach work and interpersonal situations.
- Attendance
  - *Exceeds:* Employees either meet the standard or need improvement. It is not possible to exceed on attendance. The call center environment

bases its service level success on the ability to have the appropriate resources to answer the incoming calls.

— *Meets:* This person meets handbook policy guidelines and has not exceeded his or her allotted paid time off, tardiness, or absences for the calendar year. This person is usually not late, and is here each and every day. He or she puts in the needed hours to complete the work and has no infractions greater than a verbal warning in the file. The person is consistent about bringing his or her badge to work and punches correctly each and every day. The employee is at his or her station ready to work at the scheduled shift.

— *Needs improvement:* This person does not meet handbook policy guidelines and has exceeded his or her allotted paid time off, tardiness, or absences for the calendar year. He or she often wastes time before and after the start and end of the scheduled shift. He or she frequently fails to bring his or her punch card to work or has a lot of punch or payroll errors in a two-cycle period. An employee who has received a written warning for attendance in the last six months also falls into this category.

• Commitment—Team Leader Only

— *Exceeds expectations:* This person always empowers himself or herself and his or her staff to think through problems and present facts and solutions. As a leader, this person takes responsibility for service and processing dissatisfaction and aggressively works to document, train, and implement new processes to prevent the same dissatisfaction from occurring. He or she consistently completes projects or service calls, or both, and always volunteers to participate in client and team initiatives as well as to take ownership of problem situations.

— *Meets:* This person sets the example by working to minimize errors in service situations and paper processing. This person uses his or her knowledge of the client, the team, and the processes to assist team members. He or she volunteers to participate in activities, but will also do so upon request from his or her supervisor or manager. The person has good follow-up skills and works hard to ensure closure to service or paper processes, or both.

— *Needs improvement:* This person lacks follow-through in completing tasks and projects. He or she does not consistently set the example for the team on verification processes, maintain appropriate available and idle time percentages, or propose corrective actions that would lead to preventing recurring dissatisfaction. The person does not draw participation or buy-in or create a forum to solicit ideas from the team. He or she seldom participates in client or team activities.

- Communication
  - *Exceeds expectations:* This person is a seasoned communicator in both written and verbal formats. This person consistently expresses himself or herself in a positive, professional manner, even when he or she might have an opposing point of view. He or she scores high (3.5 or better) on observer checklist guidelines. This person has excellent listening skills, which is evident in the detail with which he or she presents scenarios or solutions, or both. He or she consistently chooses words carefully when interacting with peers and management. He or she is always respectful and sensitive to others' feelings.
  - *Meets:* This person expresses himself or herself in a clear and professional manner. He or she works to make sure relevant information is communicated to the client, team, or employee. He or she appropriately escalates information to the proper resources such as supervisor and or client contact. He or she generally understands the dos and don'ts of what to say and how to say it.
  - *Needs improvement:* This person does not express himself or herself in a clear and professional manner. He or she tends to use red light words, such as *No* or, as if to place blame or sound harsh or rude, *You.* This person can also be impatient with an internal or external customer, and has a hard time consistently following Edcor's standards for providing appropriate customer service (that is, Edcor's observer guideline standards) and can be occasionally rude with the internal or external customer, or both.
- Judgment
  - *Exceeds expectations:* People either have good judgment or they do not. This person has a lot of on-the-job experience and has the knowledge that allows him or her to make decisions better than most. He or she is the best resource to contact and is usually the only person to be approached to make a decision.
  - *Meets:* This person can make good and sound decisions in daily work. He or she has a good sense of what steps need to be taken. He or she can adapt the policy question to a specific employee or situation. This person adequately empowers himself or herself to make a decision that is best for the employee or client. His or her decisions are logical and without bias.
  - *Needs improvement:* This person usually needs assistance in completing daily work. This person has a hard time choosing between A and B, as well as has a hard time deciphering what should be done or what is the right thing to do. This person makes business decisions based on (negative) personal beliefs, not on what the guidelines say.

- Leadership—Team Leader Only
  - *Exceeds expectations:* This person leads by example by accepting challenging situations that require high-level communication skills, patience, and problem resolution skills. This person arrives at work prior to the start of his or her shift and plans the day for the team. He or she gives clear direction and works off of a project plan to accomplish objectives. He or she is viewed as a nurturer of the team and client functions and is well thought of and respected within the organization.
  - *Meets:* This person assists the team and the client with any information when required or when asked. He or she motivates employees by being sincere and mature. He or she uses tools to ensure that projects, processing timelines, and company-related items are met. This person is fair in his or her approach to most situations. This person takes an active role in keeping job aids and reference materials updated.
  - *Needs improvement:* This person is still progressing on mastering leadership skills for staff planning and solutions. He or she assumes the responsibility of performing most of the work but continues to struggle with following up with the team on workloads and productivity. He or she does not consistently practice leadership skills. Often this person is swayed by personal opinion, not situational facts. He or she struggles with giving people and staff clear direction. He or she needs to build skills in motivating employees and in setting the example for others to follow.
- Problem Solving—Team Leader Only
  - *Exceeds expectations:* This person proposes viable solutions and sees them through to completion. This person does an excellent job of thinking through scenarios, coming up with two or three solutions, and recommending the best one. He or she often exceeds expectations by quickly resolving issues and communicating the results to all relevant parties. He or she is logical and committed to both correcting and preventing the same problem from recurring.
  - *Meets:* This person recognizes viable solutions and seeks input of management for feedback when needed. He or she possesses the skills to accomplish the situation within the timeframe quoted or uses the proper follow-up skills as needed when more time is needed.
  - *Needs improvement:* This person needs assistance with solving problems. He or she does not take the time to brainstorm solutions with peers or management. He or she does not follow up with customer service inquiries or fails to do so in a timely fashion. This person relies on management to drive the solutions and often brings the problems to the table.

- Productivity—Team Leader Only
  - *Exceeds expectations:* This person establishes a system to organize and create an efficient method in order to consistently meet and exceed goals and expectations for himself or herself and the team. This person coaches his or her teammates on ways to increase service and processing goals for the better of the team. He or she is committed to adding quality to his or her work by allowing time to check it or by creating a system for checks and balances.
  - *Meets:* This person and his or her team regularly meet processing goals. He or she understands that a structured work ethic is necessary for meeting these goals. This person is able to increase performance when needed to deplete backlogs and bring them within the established processing timeline required.
  - *Needs improvement:* This person struggles with meeting production goals for himself or herself or the team. He or she does not follow a system that creates organization or one that allows time for auditing work, even after the management team has made a recommendation to do so. He or she struggles with using appropriate time management skills.
- Quality
  - *Exceeds expectations:* This person takes an active role in making sure team and client materials are updated by following the process to make changes to controlled documents. He or she understands the quality tools and processes. This person has a high processing accuracy rate and communicates regularly with the team when statistical methods are not being met (that is, when applications are behind the 48-hour processing). This person develops tools that would contribute to quality within the team.
  - *Meets:* This person practices instilling quality into his or her work by being accurate (double-checking work), by utilizing team client materials, and by asking for clarification when he or she is unsure about how to proceed on a topic. He or she uses tools and references to ensure accuracy.
  - *Needs improvement:* This person generally does not add time to check work, and often there are continuous, redundant errors. He or she is often coached or receives feedback about errors in daily work.
- Quality Management—Team Leader Only
  - *Exceeds expectations:* This person consistently monitors the quality aspects of the team deliverables and takes appropriate actions to improve or correct tools or materials. He or she is a champion for quality within his or her group. He or she takes the time to review performance metrics and coaches staff on how to achieve desired results.

— *Meets:* This person is effective at resolving problems as they arise. He or she is supportive in implementing corrective or preventive actions, or both, when driven by the team supervisor. He or she has good ideas or recommendations when approached by management for feedback.

— *Needs improvement:* This person occasionally uses the quality tool to manage, monitor, and track critical processes. He or she struggles with the quality concepts and how to implement changes that affect quality.

- Resource Knowledge—Senior Agents Only
  - *Exceeds expectations:* This person steps up and provides direction or clarification about service or processing. He or she has a thorough knowledge of processing details, understands the culture of his or her clients, and can provide specifics about why one approach would be more successful than another. The staff usually relies on this person's knowledge to address questions or gray areas. He or she provides specific details when giving directions and follows up to ensure the project or task is progressing in the right direction. The client feels comfortable that this person will correctly respond to his or her concerns when presented with a question or issue.
  - *Meets:* This person understands the client's processes and procedures. He or she provides direction on how to address situations when approached by staff. He or she exhibits good delegation skills and is able to provide a better way to complete a task or handle a difficult customer. He or she handles most situations in the absence of a team leader or supervisor.
  - *Needs improvement:* This person struggles with assigning clear and specific direction when delegating daily work. He or she lacks proper follow-up, which results in the use of unnecessary energy to correct completed work and contributes to the lack of quality and quantity of work being generated. Teammates do not go to this person to resolve any questions or issues.
- Role Model and Coach—Senior Agents Only
  - *Exceeds expectations:* This person is a consistent role model and is successful at identifying areas that require additional training and coaching. He or she has an excellent understanding of when it is necessary to assist with altering workloads. He or she is always positive and is a strong advocate of the team and the client. He or she is available to assist team members with escalated calls that might involve a complaint or a service issue. He or she provides feedback to the person or team (when necessary) about what occurred, how and why a specific solution was implemented, what was the suggested

outcome, and what can be done next time to prevent or manage an escalated call.

— *Meets:* This person is available to assist the team with more complicated and detailed issue resolutions and conducts himself or herself in a positive and calm manner. He or she is successful at providing feedback or direction, or both, that is useful and makes sense to the employee. He or she often makes people feel good about their own work and gives others the motivation to continue working toward those standards and end results.

— *Needs improvement:* This person does not follow consistent team leadership and does not consistently lead by example when practicing customer service skills or reaching out to assist co-workers. He or she struggles with building team moral and is often close minded about alternate ways to solve problems.

- Staff Development—Team Leader Only
  — *Exceeds expectations:* This person is excellent at referring team members to the proper materials, resources, or checklist when confronted with a question about team or client policy. He or she promotes the utilization of proper materials and thinks through probable solutions prior to consulting someone for assistance. He or she provides honest feedback to the team in a timely and tactful manner, which creates a relationship built with trust and sincerity. This person is very accurate in assessing situations or events and is effective at documenting those thoughts in a written format.

  — *Meets:* This person is fair and honest with his or her staff. He or she works with each individual according to that person's skill set to help him or her achieve specific results. This person is open minded and encourages any type of feedback. He or she uses open communication to help work through interpersonal and knowledge based scenarios. He or she has a genuine and optimistic approach.

  — *Needs improvement:* This person often has minimal skills for working with people in a manner that motivates and stimulates. He or she has the interest of the team and client in mind, but has a hard time being effective in this area. This person tends to focus on the person, not the situation.

- Technology
  — *Exceeds expectations:* This person is extremely successful at applying technology to assist with performing his or her job. He or she presents technical solutions that would reduce time and effort and enable the team or client to focus on other areas. He or she is very knowledgeable about his or her client's solutions. The team views this person as a help desk resource for troubleshooting technology problems.

— *Meets:* This person has a good understanding of the technology solution or tools his or her client uses to service the customer or employees. This person often understands how to apply client knowledge to the specific client software. He or she practices using different software programs and shows interest in learning this aspect of his or her job function.

— *Needs improvement:* This person is only interested in using the client solution that has an impact on his or her ability to do the job. He or she is comfortable using conventional methods to track, monitor, and maintain job duties. This person may struggle with how to use technology and needs to practice it regularly to become proficient.

• Telephone Etiquette
    — *Exceeds expectations:* This person displays a high level of energy and treats every call as if it were the first. His or her telephone statistics consistently exceed the standard percentage required to maintain a low abandon rate and queue hold time. This person often receives written or verbal acknowledgement, or both, from clients and employees for exhibiting great customer service skills. He or she consistently scores high in all categories on the observer checklist (3.5 score or better).

    — *Meets:* This person consistently meets the telephone statistics standards established within the team. He or she practices good customer service skills and uses job aids to assist with maintaining those skills. He or she is receptive to feedback and coaching on alternate approaches to service-oriented situations. He or she has a pleasant disposition on the phone and is able to work with the different personalities he or she encounters. This person is able to incorporate standard observer checklist guidelines into everyday phone calls.

    — *Needs improvement:* This person struggles with controlling difficult customers. He or she often allows upset customers to alter their tone and allows them to direct the conversation. He or she does not regularly follow the observer checklist guidelines and is inconsistent with the speaking skills it sets.

Adjectives and Verbs to Describe Performance

Edcor's complete tool package to jump-start the thought process includes a list of common adjectives and verbs. A review of these words often helps an evaluator get started on an idea or assists the person in finding the right word for a description. Following are some common verbs and adjectives:

- Helpful Verbs
  - accepts
  - accomplishes
  - adapts
  - addresses
  - advances
  - advises
  - anticipates
  - applies
  - articulates
  - assists
  - assumes
  - assures
  - attempts
  - carries out
  - communicates
  - completes
  - comprehends
  - concentrates
  - conducts
  - considers
  - consults
  - contributes
  - conveys
  - cooperates
  - demonstrates
  - determines
  - develops
  - displays
  - encourages
  - enforces
  - ensures
  - excels
  - expresses
  - follows up
  - foresees
  - generates
  - gives
  - grasps
  - guides
  - handles
  - identifies
  - insures
  - maintains
  - manages
  - obtains
  - participates
  - performs
  - possesses
  - practices
  - prevents
  - prioritizes
  - recognizes
  - reinforces
  - represents
  - requires
  - resolves
  - responds
  - seeks
  - shows
  - strengthens
  - strives
  - supports
  - understands
  - uses
  - utilizes
  - verifies
  - weighs

- Helpful Adjectives
  - absolute
  - accurate
  - ambitious
  - capable
  - challenging
  - cohesive
  - competent
  - complete
  - composed
  - concise
  - considerate
  - consistent
  - constructive
  - cooperative
  - courteous
  - creative
  - dedicated
  - dependable
  - determined
  - eager
  - effective
  - efficient
  - enthusiastic
  - exceptional
  - extreme
  - fair
  - favorable
  - flexible
  - genuine
  - hands-on
  - important
  - independent
  - involved
  - knowledgeable
  - logical
  - mature
  - meaningful
  - meticulous
  - motivated
  - objective
  - open minded
  - optimistic
  - organized
  - original
  - patient
  - perceptive
  - persevering
  - pleasant
  - positive
  - practical

— precise	— resourceful	— thorough
— productive	— responsive	— unusual
— professional	— significant	— valuable
— punctual	— sincere	— versatile
— rational	— successful	— well-liked
— realistic	— supportive	— worthy
— reliable	— tactful	

Phrases and Sentences for Evaluation Writing

Following are examples of sentences that are suitable for evaluations. They may give you an idea of how to write better evaluations.

It is preferable to write as if you are talking directly to the person (in second person), rather than at or about the person (third person). Employees may respond to statements written in second person better because this style is conversational, like a talk with the employees, whereas third person might appear that you are talking at the employees or about them, as if they are not even there. Following is an example in third person:

> Adam consistently produces work of high quality. His work is complete and thorough, and he is often asked by other teams to assist in verification of payments.

Following are examples in second person:

> Adam, you consistently produce work of high quality. Your work is complete and thorough, and other teams often ask you to assist in the verification of payments.

> Joe, overall, the work you produce is very accurate. You can work toward a higher level of accuracy if you take more time to double-check your work before you move on to the next project. Often you may have keyed in data incorrectly because you were going too fast.

> Nancy, you can usually manage the basic responsibilities of this position. However, you need to focus more attention on improving your typing skills. Your ability to type is affecting the accuracy of the information you are entering into the system. In addition, I would like you to take a more active role in seeking out your team leader if you have any questions about how to assist an employee, rather than saying "I don't know" to a customer.

Susan, you present your ideas clearly and consistently to your employees and management. You have a natural ability to relate to a diverse group of people and show a great deal of patience through even challenging calls. If employees have difficulty comprehending an idea, you always take great care to present the information in more understanding terms.

Missy, you have struggled with presenting your expectations and ideas clearly to your staff and in turn this has caused some deadlines and milestones to be missed on your project. After evaluating the details, I determined some of the areas of concern stemmed from your not maintaining the weekly status meetings with your team. In the future, plan a communication meeting and agenda with your staff in advance, to ensure all the updates and deliverables are reviewed.

Bill, you are struggling with some of the basic requirements of your position. There are two areas that require immediate attention, your quality of work and your ability to provide courteous customer service. Since you have started on the team, you have had a hard time with retaining and referencing policy information. This is directly affecting your ability to give out accurate information over the phone. To help you overcome some of these concerns, take the time to document notes and make sure to ask questions to help in the process of learning the material. In addition, focus on becoming less argumentative when speaking with a customer and always make the extra effort toward customer satisfaction by offering a solution that results in a positive outcome. I would also like you to participate in a customer service refresher class when the opportunity presents itself. This can offer you a refresher on the basics skills of providing courteous customer service.

Skill Improvement

Edcor asks the evaluator to comment on principle strengths and weaknesses. It is important to give some kind of example of an overall area the employees could work on. The following phrases are examples of some of the areas in which staff could build their skills for future development:

- improve comprehension of working with multiple programs
- be consistent in quality of work
- complete training on additional programs

- manage time better
- organize work better
- develop better (or exceptional) customer service skills
- increase performance in daily quantity or work
- increase skills in problem solving and issue resolution
- increase skills in follow-through
- be open to new ideas and approaches; be flexible
- become comfortable with the technology used in your daily work
- control behavior and reactions with employees, clients, and the staff
- become more accepting of critical feedback
- accept responsibility for your actions
- minimize socializing too much on company time
- minimize taking care of personal business on company time
- develop proper time-card punching or improve attendance
- refrain from too many personal phone calls or unauthorized use of company telephones
- use your established resources to obtain information
- empower yourself appropriately to solve an issue or carry out daily tasks
- improve data entry skills
- develop policy interpretation skills
- develop your ability to answer calls from multiple programs
- develop verification skills for application processing, payment processing, and data entry
- meet deadlines and develop time management skills.

Future Skill Improvement

On the last page of Edcor's evaluation is an area that focuses on those themes that can be identified as future training needs. This is a required category on all Edcor evaluation forms because it meets an ISO 9002 quality requirement for identification of training needs to be determined for each employee. The following phrases are more detailed examples of where an employee could use more training to help in carrying out his or her position effectively:

- Learn other processes within the team or with other teams and groups.
- Take the lead or senior role on a process or project.
- Learn other clients and areas of the business.
- Assist with documenting procedures as they are created.
- Participate in new hire training or refresher training; become a coach or mentor.
- Prepare and present a training presentation for your own team on common errors or review a commonly missed policy or process.
- Assist with team training.

- Upgrade PC software application skill set.
- Have a better understanding of the technology and how it affects your position.
- Work on better assisting employees with Web or IVR questions (help desk).
- Become an expert in a particular area or about a particular client.
- Work toward becoming a client or vendor contact.
- Work on your writing skills (memo, email) and on communicating more with the client.
- Improve your ability to enter data quickly and accurately.
- Assist with creating tools that will allow you to do your job better (as well as others).
- Understand a difficult area (such as taxes, query, scanning, access database).
- Take customer service refresher training.
- Role-play training.
- Take an outside course that directly relates to your current position in which there is a skill gap.
- Work on key projects, test ideas, and so forth usually handed down by management.
- Assist with incentive ideas or the focus groups for improved environment.
- Assist with daily compilation on team statistics or monthly reports going to clients.
- Assist in the testing phases of a service launch by understanding the functionality of the system and test plan requirements.
- Consistently obtain a 3.5 score or higher when being monitored.

Key Skill Phrases

The following are a variety of phrases to describe different types of skills. Questions that would provide additional important information about the skill appear in parenthesis. Again, these phrases are to help the evaluator start the thought process. These examples are all written in the positive, but it would be easy to change the wording to fit an area that needs work.

- Communication Skills
  — demonstrates and conveys a favorable image of the organization.
- Decision Making
  — foresees the consequences of decisions.
- Dependability
  — displays a strong personal commitment to successfully completing all projects
  — is a strong and reliable member of the department

- recognizes development levels and ability levels of staff
- regularly assesses the development and effectiveness of subordinates
- cultivates strengths of subordinates.
- Evaluation Skills
  - accurately monitors performance against objectives
  - effectively rates job performance and not the individual
  - gives recognition to deserving individuals
  - initiates contests (how often? when?)
  - recognizes top performance (how?).
- Goals and Objectives
  - clearly establishes goals and purposes.
- Initiative
  - is a self-starter
  - has the ability to self-direct and self-pace
  - plans and organizes with little leadership or no assistance
  - has the quality of knowing what has to be done.
- Interpersonal Skills
  - establishes credibility with supervisors and subordinates
  - demonstrates an ability to relate.
- Leadership
  - projects self-confidence, authority, and enthusiasm
  - is a trusted leader
  - displays high energy level.
- Management
  - provides management with valid and reliable information
  - gives clear direction
  - displays an effective and productive management style.
- Maturity
  - displays maturity in handling disappointments
  - displays mature reactions
  - uses life experience in dealing with a variety of people and treats each person as an individual.
- Motivation
  - is strongly motivated to achieve optimal results
  - displays energy and vitality in performing daily responsibilities
  - develops a motivating environment
  - displays high energy and drive
  - sustains a high level of momentum
  - generates enthusiasm.
- Planning
  - effectively establishes task priorities

— effectively translates ideas into action
— develops effective strategies to attain good performance.
- Productivity
  — performs at a high energy level.
- Professionalism
  — demonstrates high standards of professional behavior.
- Resourcefulness
  — demonstrates self-reliance and resourcefulness.
- Supervisory Skills
  — maintains a work situation that stimulates the growth of individuals
  — makes certain that employees have a clear understanding of their responsibilities
  — is capable of getting work done by others
  — effectively coaches subordinates toward achievement
  — is readily accessible to subordinates
  — develops strong credibility with subordinates
  — understands different personalities and traits
  — ensures that all personnel problems are properly documented
  — takes appropriate action without offending
  — tactfully admits mistakes and errors
  — builds a team spirit
  — places a high value on time effectiveness
  — makes effective use of peak time periods
  — performs a broad range of assignments with efficiency and accuracy
  — displays flexibility in adapting to changing conditions
  — grasps the essential differences in the personalities of staff and is aware of strengths and weaknesses and manages them as individuals.
- Versatility
  — is valuable in providing back-up support for other jobs.

The following phrases pertain to qualities and characteristics of a leader:
- Personal Qualities
  — is direct in a fair and positive manner
  — follows businesslike procedures to accomplish objectives
  — presents himself or herself in a polished, poised manner and displays positive responses to negative situations
  — uses humor constructively
  — displays high energy and a pleasant demeanor.
- Performance Qualities
  — develops positive realistic expectations
  — sets high standards for himself or herself and staff

- prevents personnel conflicts; mediates for others; prevents conflicts from reducing productivity
- responds quickly to feedback and acts in a timely manner
- maintains a high degree of involvement with his or her staff, team leaders, and agents
- makes sound decisions in the absence of a manager and executive staff
- forecasts and anticipates call volume, scheduling, turnover, and so forth
- sets up goals for determining courses of actions for his or her staff
- effectively develops and provides direction to individuals, department, and organization to obtain goals and objectives
- effectively motivates staff.
- Responsibilities and Duties
  - maintains proper scheduling
  - provides coverage or a plan for coverage if someone is scheduled to be off work
  - reviews phone report data for scheduling and identifying problem areas
  - reviews productivity reports and communicates the results with staff
  - reviews staffing overview and oversees the assignments of new hires
  - assists in problem solving of program issues and working closely with other departments
  - prepares proper documentation for payroll if needed
  - mediates conflict
  - meets daily and project deadlines
  - meets with staff to coach and counsel
  - reviews phone reports
  - monitors abandonment rate and responds accordingly
  - manages team leaders
  - ensures that department policies and procedures are followed
  - creates and suggests training programs and tools to increase productivity, performance, and overall job knowledge
  - offers solutions to problems
  - creates a team environment in which the person's staff enjoys working with him or her, each other, and the company.
- Development Responsibilities
  - provides leadership and direction to team leaders and agents
  - conveys expectations and goals in writing when possible, and uses performance logs
  - communicates thoughts and ideas, visions, and expectations

— maintains and is familiar with all team statistics
— assists supervisors in determining what areas are in need of improvement and implements creative and innovative solutions; follows up to make sure changes have taken place
— makes sure 60-day evaluations and performance improvement plans are completed in a timely manner and that follow-up was done if necessary
— meets with staff daily to review plans, changes, and things that are happening for the week
— meets with manager weekly to receive direction for his or her program
— encourages and schedules team meetings, training, and incentives (depending on call volume)
— develops programs to improve the effectiveness of the department and the overall operation of the organization
— plans to meet with his or her manager or director regarding the performance of his or her shift
— develops and monitors productivity standards and assists in managing quality
— reviews productivity reports
— manages the quality process.

Putting It Together

Once the evaluator has completed the rough draft, it is crucial to read it aloud as if you are the person receiving the review. By doing this, you may catch errors or awkward phrases that you did not realize were even there. Finally, if you have the resources, make sure a second pair of eyes has proofread for content and grammatical errors, especially if it is your first time writing an evaluation. Remember, the content of the review is confidential, so choose a resource that is appropriate and at the right level to review the information you have written. Also remember your management team may read the review you write and get an impression of your skill and ability to offer appropriate feedback. So although you might think of your role as only the evaluator, think again, and write the review as if it were you under review. It may well be.

Questions for Discussion

1. What is the philosophy of performance evaluations in this call center?
2. How does your performance evaluation philosophy compare with this one?

3. What changes would you make to your system and why?
4. What are the key aspects in building an evaluation process for your company? What tools can you develop or provide that will keep evaluator and evaluatees motivated through the whole process?

The Authors

Tanya Koons is the general manager and a member of the executive management team at Edcor. She has over 10 years' experience in call centers, operations, and employee incentive and development. Koons manages the shared services group of HR Services. Her responsibilities include recruiting, training, quality, HR policy, and incentives as well as facilities. Koons also holds a key role as the management representative for Edcor's ISO 9002 quality program. She has the authority and responsibility to develop, implement, and maintain the quality standards outlined in the universally recognized ISO 9000 quality series. Edcor obtained its registration in June 2000 under Koons' leadership as the lead facilitator. Koons is also a certified lead auditor and manages Edcor's internal audit team, and she heads up the ISO Steering Committee, where policy is driven and corrective and preventive actions are monitored for the entire company. Koons is a 1990 graduate of Michigan State University, with a bachelor of science degree in business. She can be reached at Edcor, 3937 Campus Drive, Pontiac, MI 48341; phone: 248.836.1310; email: tkoons@Edcor.com.

Jonetta Pettway is a manager at Edcor and is a member of the HR Services group, specifically overseeing the company's new hire and ongoing training needs. She has held several operational roles within the Edcor organization and brings her expertise as both a client and a staff manager when identifying and developing training needs. Pettway is also a lead internal auditor and an ISO Steering Committee member. She plays a key role in driving change and maintaining a positive spirit among employees within the call center. Pettway is a 1986 graduate of Northwood University with a bachelor of arts in management and marketing.

High Touch, High Yield: Creating the Optimal Service Experience for Your Most Profitable Customers

Intuit Inc.

Reed Engdahl and Jarrett Perdue

This case study explores how an inbound call center recruited, trained, and developed a select group of high-potential agents to service high-revenue customers. The call center's goals were as follows:
- *increase revenue and product penetration*
- *provide customers with a full-service business consultant*
- *improve customer retention.*

The case study details how training and organizational development played a key role and illustrates the financial impact and return-on-investment from the performance improvement intervention.

Organizational Profile

Intuit Inc., the makers of Quicken, QuickBooks, and TurboTax software, is a leader in e-finance, including financial software and Web-based financial services for consumers and small businesses. Founded in 1983 and incorporated in 1993, the company's mission is to revolutionize how business and individuals manage their financial lives, with the goal of making the complicated chore of managing our customers' books easier, helping save them time and money.

Intuit, based in Mountain View, California, operates a number of business units to support these products, one of which is the Financial Supplies Group that sells custom products such as checks, envelopes, tax forms, and other paper products specially designed to work

This case was prepared to serve as a basis for discussion rather than to illustrate either effective or ineffective administrative and management practices.

with Quicken and QuickBooks software. This business unit operates an inbound-only call center in Fredericksburg, Virginia, a city of 25,000 between Washington, D.C., and Richmond, Virginia. The call center is staffed with full-time agents year-round, but the workforce nearly doubles with a temporary workforce during the autumn and winter months to coincide with higher sales levels near the beginning of the year. During these peak months, many consumers and business owners change financial management software programs so as not to disrupt accounting methods midyear, driving higher call volumes into the call center. Sales of paper products increase accordingly when more consumers switch to Quicken and QuickBooks, and as current or renewing users need to purchase tax forms to comply with year-end IRS filing requirements.

The Fredericksburg area contains a primarily semi-educated, semi-rural workforce, and since it is located over 50 miles from both Washington and Richmond, it has only just recently begun to attract a professional workforce seeking moderately priced housing who is also willing to commute up to two hours in either direction. The area also has two major call centers and one smaller call center, employing over 2,000 agents. Because these other call centers require their agents to possess either certifications or financial security requirements, they typically have a slightly higher pay scale and can offer employment year-round. While the Intuit permanent workforce meets and exceeds the requirements of the job, and often stays at Intuit for the casual working environment and better benefits typically found in a high-tech company, the seasonal workforce, that can account for 50 percent of the workforce at its peak, can be made up of uncommitted, unskilled workers who know they are employed for only a finite period of time.

Issues That Triggered the Need for the Elite Group

The call center had a great disparity of skills and experience because of the mix of permanent and temporary employees due to turnover and seasonal employment, and the learning curve necessary to become proficient as a sales associate. At the same time, the call center was transforming itself from a customer service center that primarily focused on order taking to a sales and service center responsible for generating revenue through sales and consultation to Quicken and QuickBooks users. Many of the permanent employees had been hired to perform only basic customer service skills, and they lacked the skill or desire to become salespeople. Finally, once they had mastered the basics of the sales associate job, they had little opportunity to acquire and practice additional skills since no formal career track existed. All sales associates held the same job grade regardless of tenure or quality of service, whether basic or excellent. Therefore, there was little incentive to move beyond the basics. As a result, despite many efforts to introduce sales skills and techniques to the associates, the center's internal quality assurance team continued to report that a minority of all sales associates regularly used some sort of sales skill on their calls.

Technology

The business unit had recently developed a ranking system to identify customers by the amount of revenue they spent on supplies with the company each year. When an inbound call came through the system and the computer telephony interface, the customer's contact and past purchase information was matched against a database, and that ranking could be delivered to the agent's desktop. While this functionality was in place, the Financial Supplies Group had yet to leverage the information to change the call routing. As a result, a call from a high-revenue customer could be delivered to a rather new, seasonal agent, resulting in an inconsistent sales and service experience.

The Business Opportunity

The call center was not in a position to offer the continuity of experience and the quality necessary to achieve long-term revenue growth. The challenge was to create a new dynamic: Match our high-revenue customers with sales associates who were motivated to learn the sales skills necessary to lead the transformation from a customer service center to a sales and service center.

To achieve that goal, the project team established a project plan to reengineer the customer experience for the high-revenue customers. First, sales associates would be trained to offer a high-touch experience to the customer segment where it would have the greatest impact. Highest revenue clients would have consistent, professional experiences, increasing the probability of their calling again for future purchases. Second, these same associates would seek to tap into the revenue potential of this customer segment. Through consultative sales techniques, the team would attempt to increase revenue on each call by 10 percent.

Project Plan

The project was divided into two components: selecting and training personnel and setting up the desktop and information systems.

Personnel

No phase of the project plan was more critical than recruiting the right people from the current staff of full-time employees.

First, the project team sought the right leadership. Part of the investment was the realization that a huge amount of daily hands-on coaching, training, and reinforcement would be required to maintain the momentum of this sales and service team. For this reason, a sales trainer was assigned to the project for the first three months to act in the capacity of performance consultant and project manager.

The other leadership component was the team supervisor who was selected for the following traits:

- demonstrated commitment to the management philosophy of Intuit as described in the value, "It's the People" (one of Intuit's core operating values)
- the ability to operate in a nontraditional supervisory role with a customer-centric focus, not a process-centric focus
- the ability to coach and teach
- a clear communicator with stamina and enthusiasm who could galvanize the team in pursuit of project goals
- an expert salesperson in her own right.

In recruiting for the sales associates, the qualities that best defined a high-touch associate were as follows:

- a willingness to learn and a desire to grow professionally
- a clear verbal communication style
- a genuine desire to help each customer
- the ability to work an extended shift to accommodate daily training time.

Because this was a special project team, the pay grade for the team members would not change.

RECRUITMENT. The recruiting process began with an extensive review of all personnel based on the feedback of the quality assurance staff, identifying those employees who exhibited a willingness to be coached and a genuine empathy for the customers. The next step was a statistical review of sales results, looking for trends in cross selling and product penetration. In addition, the project team asked the center's nine team supervisors for recommendations based on the competency requirements to identify the seasonal and new associates who may have been overlooked during the first pass of historical data.

Two center-wide email broadcasts were also delivered to generate employee interest for this new effort. Teaser messages asked the following:

"Is your call quality smoking?"

"Do you cross-sell like a champ?"

"Do your customers demand to speak to a supervisor so they can rave about what great service you give?"

"Do you provide Five-Star service on the phone?"

"Do you go above and beyond to help each customer?"

"Do you enjoy learning and practicing new sales techniques to improve your skills?"

We're starting a new sales and service project team that will constantly be experimenting with new ways to sell with integrity and new ways to WOW our customers with outstanding service. If this sounds like you, then you may be the perfect candidate for the job. Just reply to this e-mail so we can talk.

The email generated responses from 40 sales associates, both from the year-round and the seasonal staff, who expressed interest in the program because of their desire and willingness to try something new and challenging, despite the realization that their compensation would not change. All candidates participated in a one-hour interview that screened for sales background, small business knowledge and orientation, willingness to learn, flexibility, drive and enthusiasm, and a customer-centric approach to work. The interview questions (and desired behaviors the question was designed to uncover) were as follows:

- How many teams have you been on? What changes did you experience moving from one team to another? (flexibility)
- What is the biggest change you have seen since working in this center? (positive attitude)
- What are two different approaches you use to sell? What makes you choose one over the other? (sales aptitude)
- What kinds of sales situations give you the most trouble? Which are the most satisfying? (customer centric)
- What do you like best about your current position? (customer centric)
- When have you had to go against general feelings or policies to accomplish a goal? Tell me about it. (innovation)
- What way have you found to make your job more rewarding? (self-esteem)
- Can you give me examples of job experiences that you felt were especially satisfying or dissatisfying?
- Describe when you worked the hardest and felt the greatest sense of accomplishment.

- How do you organize your day? (time management)
- How do you deal with an irate customer? (self-control)
- How do you show your customers that you are listening to them? (listening and consultation skills)
- How good are your listening skills? How do you know?
- What factors do you consider most important when you evaluate your success overall? Your job performance?

The interviews culminated in the selection of 12 candidates who were offered positions on the team. In addition to those 12, there were 12 to 15 sales associates that were well-qualified and very interested, but were unable to commit to the work schedule.

TEAM PROFILE. Table 1 illustrates the job experience of those candidates chosen for the team. While the candidates' years of experience as employees in the call center varied greatly, their years in a small business or customer service environment, or both, were unusually extensive.

Training

The new team was trained in two different stages:

STAGE ONE: ORIENTATION AND INITIATION. A weeklong training and orientation took place to initiate the 12 associates. The syllabus included the following topics:

- *A broad overview of the supplies business:* This included not just a thorough overview of the products and supplies the Financial Supplies Group offered, but also an overview of the major competitors, their products, and their prices. While research shows that many of Intuit's supplies customers are very loyal, it also showed that customers will shop around for better prices and other services. Making the sales associates knowledgeable of the competitive landscape ensured that they could speak professionally to the customers about products and prices and, if necessary, provide appropriate discounts.
- *An introduction to the customer ranking system:* The new team also had to know who these high-revenue customers were, specifically their

Table 1. Years of experience.

	Center Tenure	Small Business Environment	Customer Service Environment
Average	1.8	6.8	10.3
Total	21.8	81.5	124

buying habits and motives and the industries in which they worked. The team learned how often they ordered, what types of products they typically ordered and in what quantities, and, more important, the products they did not order, giving the team an idea of how to better meet their needs. By giving the team the information about whom they were selling to, they learned not just how to meet the customers' needs, but also felt more confident and assured when making product recommendations.

- *Vision building:* One key to the team's success was "working" like a team to achieve success as one, not as a group of individuals. In order to envision their success, a key part of the first and last days revolved around creating a vision statement for themselves. While this took up time, the vision that the team created for themselves, and felt wedded to, was often referred to months later and used to energize them if they felt a goal was not being achieved.

- *The questioning sales model:* To learn to perform like consultants, the sales associates learned that the best way to meet customer needs was to ask them about their business requirements. Unlike the balance of the associates in the sales and service center who have learned to sell by offering products, this new team was trained to uncover customer desires by asking a number of business and product usage questions, such as "What accounting problems did you face before you began using QuickBooks?" and "What is your biggest bookkeeping challenge?" The associates were initially hesitant about using this technique because they did not feel fully qualified to help a small business make decisions, but as their questioning techniques improved and as their sales and recommendations improved, they gradually gained the confidence needed to perfect the techniques.

- *The psychology of success:* The team learned that success is as much a state of mind as anything else. The associates had to be taught that they could both achieve anything they set their minds to and were already successful if they felt it in their heart. Using some positive mental attitude techniques, the team members gradually began to feel that they could achieve anything, and subsequently did achieve sales and product penetration well beyond what they had ever achieved before. Looking back at the initial training, the project team feels that the module that focused on building self-confidence and esteem may have been more important than any other training component.

- *Handling objections:* To many of the team members, an objection was often viewed as a personal rejection. They had to be taught that objections really mean, "I don't understand why I should buy this product or service." Once the team learned that an objection was nothing more than an open door to continue attempting to sell to the customer, they overcame many initial customer objections and learned the technique to improving their closing ratio.

- *A day in the life of a small business:* While some of the sales associates on the new team had worked in a small business, none of them had ever owned a small business. Therefore, they needed to understand the financial and operational pressures small businesses faced every day. They learned some basic accounting terms, record-keeping requirements, and decisions that business owners face when evaluating purchases and suppliers. This background ultimately helped them understand what questions to ask, see which products fit different businesses, and identify the customers' buying motives.

- *QuickBooks:* While it would seem obvious that the employees would already have extensive knowledge of the QuickBooks software, the reality was that the Financial Supplies Group received very few calls for software technical support; and if they did, the calls were rerouted to the QuickBooks call centers. However, teaching this team some basics of the software proved to be helpful when the new team needed to sell the customer on the need for a product. Because the associates knew exactly how their products integrated with Intuit software, they could exude a great deal of confidence when promoting their supplies products. This, naturally enough, built larger and more frequent sales.

STAGE TWO: ONGOING TRAINING. After the first week of training, the team was ready to begin its work. In order to make the training stick, however, the team began daily hour-long reinforcement and training sessions. These sessions, from 9 a.m. to 10 a.m. before the normal eight-hour shift, were designed to accomplish the following:
- introduce or share new material and sales tactics
- set revenue goals and check progress
- reenergize the team for the sales day ahead.

For the first three months, the team was also introduced to a six-part sales model that emphasized questioning and probing techniques, uncovering buying motives, and leading the client toward a positive buying decision.

Looking back at the project, the project team believes that the key to making the orientation training stick was the daily reinforcement of material and the continual learning. Had the team received no additional training after the first week, it is likely that 90 percent of the material would have been lost over time, and the project would have eventually failed. In fact, on the few days when the morning training session had to be postponed, sales production for that day (which included the same number of staffed phone hours) was always lower.

Environment.

Several broad environmental changes were made to facilitate the effort.

LOCATION OF TEAM. The team was stationed slightly apart from the main sales floor. By placing the members together, yet somewhat insulated from the general population, they exerted a continuous, reinforcing influence on one another during the day, while also remaining somewhat outside of the influence of the rest of the center (which was not nearly as sales focused at the time).

SCHEDULING. Schedules were built for the team members to match the customer call volume and still accommodate the need for the daily training sessions.

MONITORING CALL QUALITY. The responsibility for tracking and maintaining call quality standards moved from a centralized quality assurance group to the team level. The team leader remotely monitored and coached less on the normal mechanics of the call and more on the content of the morning training session. Monitoring and coaching also focused on the sales associates' ability to recognize and act upon buying motive (that is, the use of "problem" and "solution" questions to create the urgency to buy) and on effective matching of supplies and software products with the customers' industry and business needs.

OTHER FACTORS. Team members were withdrawn from most centerwide special project work in order to maintain their focus on sales and customer retention. Also, the team was excused from daily and monthly sales contests due to the likelihood of winning all revenue-based contests. Different contests were developed, however, within the team to keep the associates motivated to achieve their goals.

Results

Four months after the team began servicing these high-revenue customers, the results were evaluated on the following parameters:
- average order size for the high-revenue customers (Not all high-revenue calls went to the team. Other agents in the center also sold to this population, but they did not receive the same training.)
- items per order
- average order size for the other customers (Since call volume from the high-revenue customers varied, the team was placed in other call splits to ensure that adequate service levels were maintained.)
- number of software units sold per week

- number of ancillary products sold per week
- percent of revenue contribution
- product penetration.

While one of the project goals was to increase customer retention, buying cycles necessitated using a longer time frame in which to measure progress.

The project was evaluated by measuring results from calls and orders from the high-revenue customer population placed with the project team in comparison with calls from this same customer base placed with other teams. That way the effect the training and management had on revenue could be isolated.

- *Average order size: high-revenue customers:* The average order size from the high-revenue customers increased by 11.8 percent.
- *Average order size: all other customers:* Although the focus of the project was the high-revenue customer, the average order size for the team from all the other customers also increased by 12.3 percent.
- *Items per order:* The number of items purchased on the average order also increased 23 percent.
- *Number of software units sold per week:* While the team made up less than 10 percent of the call center population, it generated 48 percent of the software unit sales. This is testament to the team's ability to improve product penetration when the associate functions as a consultant, recommending products specific to the customer's industry and practices.
- *Number of ancillary products sold per week.* The number of ancillary products, such as envelopes and business forms, also increased to 20 percent of the revenue due to successful cross-selling techniques.
- *Percent of revenue contribution:* The project team, which accounted for less than 10 percent of the center, generated up to 15 percent of the revenue.
- *Product penetration:* The project team was able to make significant inroads into introducing other products to customers. Fifty percent of the team's revenue came from products other than checks, while the general call center population had 38 percent of its revenue from noncheck products.

Conclusions

The project team drove significant incremental revenue, not just with the high-revenue customers as planned, but also with the rest of the customer base. Because of the revenue generated across all segments of the client base, it is possible to see the potential impact the training could have on the rest of the call center.

Also critical to the success of the project was the practice of re-inforcing the initial and ongoing training techniques every day. Effective sales techniques were learned by actually applying them, not through studying in the abstract. The daily classroom time created a valuable forum in which to practice over and over again.

The project was also an effective change process. The individuals on the team have grown in their knowledge, skills, beliefs, and expectations. They are satisfied with their work, and are motivated to continue building their skills and knowledge base. They see application of their learning from this effort in both their personal and professional lives. While they have also felt burnout for the first 45 days due to the keen listening, probing, analytical, and sales skills they invest in their calls, they are growing as professionals. Finally, they feel they have a future with Intuit and have remained at the center to participate in similar projects, feeling that the company has made a real and lasting investment in their growth. Turnover among this group is much lower than that in the other teams, largely due to each party's commitment to success.

In the end, the project demonstrated that focused training, when reinforced every day, may contribute to sizable, measurable financial results.

Questions for Discussion

1. How did this call center recruit and train a group of high-potential agents to service high-revenue clients?
2. What is the definition of high-revenue clients?
3. How did training and organizational development play a key role in creating a financial impact and return-on-investment?
4. What were the special considerations used to select the high-potential agents?
5. How could you use this business and training model in your call center?

The Authors

Reed Engdahl recently served as training manager for Intuit's Financial Supplies Group in Fredericksburg, Virginia, and was with the company since 1999. Prior to that, he spent four years as training manager at the American Petroleum Institute and 10 years in training and other functions with Mobil Oil. He has published and spoken on a number of petroleum industry training issues in the United States and the Middle East. Engdahl has a business degree from the University of

Illinois at Urbana-Champaign. He can be reached at 9523 Oak Stream Court, Fairfax Station, VA 22039; phone: 703.690.6718; email: Rengdahl@cox.rr.com.

Jarrett Perdue is a trainer in his fifth year with Intuit. He graduated, a Phi Beta Kappa, from Mary Washington College, in Fredericksburg, Virginia, where he studied anthropology and classics. He also worked developing multicultural public school curricula for Chinle Unified School District #24, on the Navajo Nation, in Chinle, Arizona.

Measuring Training Effectiveness in a Call Center

A Wireless Voice and Data Services Company

Michael Voellinger

This case study is to help readers accurately measure call center training effectiveness in a tiered, business services environment. It presents a model that includes measuring representatives against expectations, up sell and cross sell measurement of products and offers, and customer base impact analysis. Please note, this case is data centric in nature. While many factors influence call center performance, the model is based purely on the capture of key indicators that directly relate to training effectiveness and the application of those indicators in a comprehensive reporting model.

The author demonstrates a straightforward method of capturing the tangible effects of training delivery, specifically focusing on the financial impacts and transactional performance. The use of simple call center metrics combined with financial reporting can provide a clear picture of employees after training and of the training program itself.

Background

The challenge faced in this wireless voice and data services organization, and the basis for this case, focuses on one simple concept: understanding the impact of training delivery. While the statement is small, the impact is huge. The company is challenged with double-digit growth in almost every category. Call volumes have risen astronomically. The impacts of e-commerce and e-servicing are not yet understood.

The company has traditionally reported on key indicators in a call center environment. It reports service levels, handle times, abandon rates, and speed of answer. While these numbers are critical, they represent only part of the entire story. In the age of double-digit growth from quarter to quarter, it needs more than a set of indicators.

Like most businesses, this organization has been traditionally focused on the delivery of world-class service in a call center environment, to a mixed consumer base. This is a broad statement of purpose, and it presents three key challenges. First, what is world-class service, and second, what customer experience is it trying to deliver? Finally, what drives all this? Initially, training. Training is a key driver for culture and expectation, both factors in delivering meaningful care. World-class service in most call centers has been defined by the assumed customer expectation: Answer 80 percent of your calls in 20 seconds or less. What happens when you answer 100 percent of your calls in 21 seconds? In this company's assessments of its call centers it found that one key question had yet to be answered: "What do these numbers mean to the customer, to our organization, and to our profitability?" There was a perceived method, based on historical practices, for measuring performance in the organization. Known as *dashboard,* the method was a compilation of metrics and measurements consolidated into one reporting package. While this dashboard mentality did capture key indicators, it did not answer the question of effectiveness. And it certainly did not touch the impact that training has on any of this!

Defining and delivering the customer experience is another challenge. All of the call centers work directly with individual, nonbusiness consumers (known as pure consumers) as well as with other purchasers such as small and large businesses, corporations, and governments. This case study focuses on three of the nine call centers. The experience and expectation of the pure consumer is radically different from that of the corporation. How do you measure each segment in a "diluted" reporting environment? (That is, how do you measure customer satisfaction for a consumer and a corporation based on the same metrics, when the two have different drivers and where "acceptable" service levels are the same for consumers as they are for the corporate customer?). And most important, how does training fit in?

Organizational Profile

The organization is a premier provider of wireless voice and data services, servicing the entire United States, with additional services providing international usage. It has over 5,000 employees nationally, with nine call centers, not including vendor support.

The initiative to measure training effectiveness is enterprisewide. Traditionally, its growth has covered up any inefficiencies in the company. While it is great to be able to overlook a better process due to that kind of growth and revenue, it does not prevent the company from eventually having to answer to the balance sheet. Efficiencies gained from training are monumental. They have an impact on almost every facet of the business, from the capability to deliver the customer experience to creating a supportive corporate culture. A well-trained employee is armed with tools, including knowledge and empowerment. Fueling every successful organization is an employee base with passion for what it does. That passion begins the first day the employee enters the center, sits down at a desk, and begins a journey toward excellence. Most employees are aimed at this goal, being passionate about what they do. Effective training will bolster that energy, whereas ineffective training will eventually diminish that passion in frustration and disillusionment. This company, thankfully, has asked the question, "Is our training effective?"

There was a clear decision made at the executive level to make measurement a priority. The author's group, specifically, was given the task of developing a big picture view of the business. This included key indicator dashboards, financial summaries, and return-on-investment (ROI) measurements. Training effectiveness was the pivotal measurement. If the group was missing the mark on delivering critical knowledge, there was no hope of delivering its experience. The results from all of this reporting did not accomplish the task. The results need to point at specific levers to be pushed or pulled, or specific pieces of the business that need attention or deserve accolades.

Key Players

The organizational structure, shown in figure 1, played a key role in the company's ability to measure. The training group is part of the company's operational structure, not its human resources group. There is alignment and communication with HR, but as a whole the training group resides in the functional units directly.

The implementation of all measurements happened at the analytical level, with executive direction. Figure 2 shows the structure of the organization.

The metrics group was allowed to work directly with leadership in each functional area. That freedom gave the group full latitude in the development of what was truly important to each unit, capturing the real front-line drivers. The metrics group is made up of (currently) senior business analysts and production analysts. They remain

Figure 1. Organizational structure for operational and functional groups.

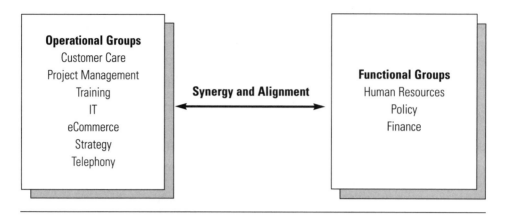

Operational Groups
Customer Care
Project Management
Training
IT
eCommerce
Strategy
Telephony

Synergy and Alignment

Functional Groups
Human Resources
Policy
Finance

Figure 2. Organizational structure for operational leadership.

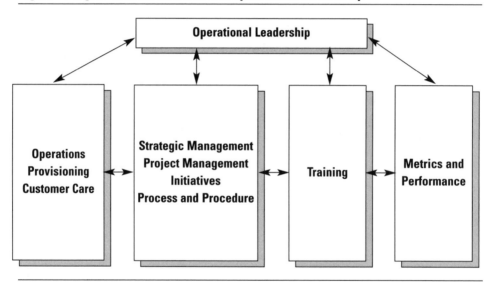

Operational Leadership

**Operations
Provisioning
Customer Care**

**Strategic Management
Project Management
Initiatives
Process and Procedure**

Training

**Metrics and
Performance**

independent of each business unit, almost in a referee capacity. The analysts are not tied to individual centers or groups and are autonomous in the organization. This is critical. Many call centers have a group of analysts, mostly for scheduling and routing, that is also responsible for measuring call center performance. This tie to the call centers allows for some padding to occur in the results, and that practice happens every day. Another benefit to having a separate measurement group is that these analysts offer a fresh set of eyes on processes and data that they are not directly involved in.

In this company, analysts must understand the center and its processes from the point of view of call center representatives. This knowledge is critical to developing the real drivers to identify good and bad business. A call center director may inquire about cost per call or percent of customer base calling over a given period of time. The representative, however, may be engrossed in how many times he or she duplicates entries into systems that may not work correctly. The representatives focus on how many times a customer they have just touched—whether by voice contact, email, or in person—will call back. These are the tangible measurements of success.

This group was the ideal place to measure training. It touched every center, the leadership team, the executive decision makers, and the front-line employee. It was in a position to tie all of these pieces together. The National Systems and Performance group (analysts) decided to start with training effectiveness because it had one of the biggest impacts on the company.

Key Issues and Events

Finances—the quest to answer for the company's financial results— was the real driver for this entire initiative. Training metrics became the center of attention by virtue of impact. The company was spending a sizable amount of money per employee to train and develop, but had no practical mechanism to identify the success of that program.

The budgeting process was also a catalyst. In capital expenditures for fiscal year 2000, training was a large cost center. There was an implied understanding that it was necessary based on the company's growth, but no real understanding of what that money represented in performance. The question was repeatedly asked, "What is the net effect of reducing the training budget by 10 percent?" There was no answer. This had to change! The initiative was again the focus of management and leadership.

Target Population

The implementation of the company's training effectiveness model has been applied to the groups of people using this structure, as figure 3 shows.

Even though development and production of the actual metrics are derived from the performance group, the audience runs through the key positions directly engaging the center itself. Those being

Figure 3. Target population of the training effectiveness model.

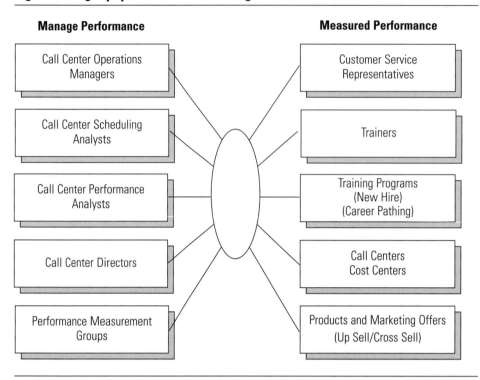

| Manage Performance | Measured Performance |

Call Center Operations Managers

Call Center Scheduling Analysts

Call Center Performance Analysts

Call Center Directors

Performance Measurement Groups

Customer Service Representatives

Trainers

Training Programs (New Hire) (Career Pathing)

Call Centers Cost Centers

Products and Marketing Offers (Up Sell/Cross Sell)

measured, on the right side of the diagram, are all subject to the analysis. The model can be easily modified to fit almost any group or function. The results data can be drilled up or down, ranging from measurement of one training group to measurement of an entire nation of call centers.

Action Items

For this example, we will assume Company X has three call centers. Each call center will be delivering the same training, but the classes will be taught by different trainers in each location. We will also assume that the training costs and employee costs are flat across all three centers.

There are two distinct steps in implementing the training effectiveness measurement. Step one is to compile the ROI calculation for each center, and step two rolls up the individual centers for a national, or companywide view.

Step One: Compile the Results for One Call Center

This step demonstrates how to assemble our model for our call center. The model, when complete, is as shown in table 1.

Following is a description of how to prepare each component of the table. Table 2 shows the compilation of some standard information on business assumptions that are key to the model. These metrics are flexible to a degree, and some of them may be a best guess.

Not all ACD systems can report with the same sophistication, so populate as much as you can. The following definitions are used for these assumptions:

- *FTE,* full-time employee
- *cost per IVR hit,* caller reaches the automated response system, but does not connect with a representative
- *cost per call,* total average cost per complete call into the center
- *average cost per page view,* average cost for an employee to utilize infrastructure (that is, look up a rate plan reference page on an intranet)
- *average calls per resolution,* the average number of times a subscriber would call the center to resolve one issue (such as an incorrect bill)
- *one call resolution savings,* money saved if average call (or issue) was resolved in a single attempt, with no callbacks.

Table 3 captures some fundamental information about the training itself and the associated costs, which will be especially critical in the ROI calculation. For these calculations, the new hire FTE is the number of employees being trained. The number of classes is the new hire FTE divided by the standard class size. The curriculum attrition rate is the number of employees who were terminated based on the inability to comprehend or complete the training materials, such as tests.

Table 4 captures the performance at a 30-day benchmark, post-training. We have identified the performance expectation and measured the current period, or actual performance. The performance expectations will vary from center to center or even by company. Most call-taking groups can identify these numbers very quickly. This is a ramp model (that is, there is analysis of the group at specific segments of time after training). Your expectations should reflect tenure, in this case at 30 days.

With this table, the metrics take shape. Consider handle time as the example for the calculation. The same method applies to all the items in table 5. If there are different measures of performance in your business, plug them in. The model will still provide a clear indication of training performance.

Table 1. The complete model for one call center.

Business Assumptions	Cost ($)
Cost per FTE (hour)	13.50
Cost per FTE (minute)	0.225
Cost per IVR hit/abandon	1.39
Cost per call	3.84
Average cost/page view	0.01
Average calls/resolution	2.3
One call resolution revenue savings	4.99

New Hire Training	Current Period
New hire FTE	76
Number of classes	3.04
Average employees per class	25
Total hours	12,160
Total hours per FTE	160
Attrition rate	2%
Job abandon rate	1%
Curriculum attrition	2%
Total trainer cost per hour	$24.50
Curriculum deployment cost	$100,000.00
Curriculum delivery cost	$50,000.00
Curriculum delivery cost (FTE)	$1,973.60
Curriculum development hours	0

Posttrain Ramp Metrics, 30 Days	Performance Expectation	Current Period
Occupancy	65	63
Call volume	630-850	686
Handle time	5.5	5.6
Abandon rate	5	5
After call work	2.2	2.19
Quality score	84	86
Page views	1,890-2,550	1,979
Work hours (average)	62	64
One call resolution %	10	8.4

ROI Calculation	Current Period
Training delivery cost	$1,973.60
Handle time deviation	$(84.89)
Abandon revenue	$-
After call revenue	$1.54
Page view deviation	$(0.89)
Work hours	$27.00
One call resolution revenue	$(96.94)
ROI calculation	−8%

Posttrain Ramp Metrics, 60 Days	Performance Expectation	Current Period
Occupancy	73	75
Call volume	850-1050	900
Handle time	4.3	4.1
Abandon rate	4	4
After call work	2	2
Quality score	88	90
Page views	1,700-2,100	1,850
Work hours (average)	65	75
One call resolution %	15	16

ROI Calculation	Current Period
Training delivery cost	$1,973.60
Handle time deviation	$174.15
Abandon revenue	$-
After call revenue	$-
Page view deviation	$0.80
Work hours	$30.40
One call resolution revenue	$79.49
ROI calculation	14%

Table 1. The complete model for one call center (continued).

Posttrain Ramp Metrics, 90 Days	Performance Expectation	Current Period
Occupancy	85	86
Call volume	1,000–1,200	1,175
Handle time	3.6	3.5
Abandon rate	3	2.77
After call work	1.5	1.64
Quality score	95	98
Page views	1,000–1,200	1,050
Work hours (average)	68	71.3
One call resolution %	10	12

ROI Calculation	Current Period
Training delivery cost	$1,973.60
Handle time deviation	$95.18
Abandon revenue	$3.76
After call revenue	$(37.01)
Page view deviation	$8.40
Work hours	$44.55
One call resolution revenue	$207.55
ROI calculation	16%

Time	30 Days	60 Days	90 Days
TCPF	$1,973.60	$1,973.60	$1,973.60
TDD	$(154.18)	$284.84	$322.42
CE	−8%	14%	16%

Note:
TCPF, total cost per full-time employee: Identify total cost of training, divided by number of employees trained.
TDD, Identify total deviation per identified driver, then total deviation.
CE, cost-effectiveness: Finalize cost effectiveness calculation, CE = TDD/TCPF.

Table 2. Business assumptions.

	Cost ($)
Cost per FTE (hour)	13.50
Cost per FTE (minute)	0.225
Cost per IVR hit/abandon	1.39
Cost per call	3.84
Average cost/page view	0.01
Average calls/resolution	2.3
One call resolution revenue savings	4.99

Table 3. Training information.

New Hire Training	Current Period
New hire FTE	76
Number of classes	3.04
Average employees per class	25
Total hours	12,160
Total hours per FTE	160
Attrition rate	2%
Job abandon rate	1%
Curriculum attrition	2%
Total trainer cost per hour	$24.50
Curriculum deployment cost	$100,000.00
Curriculum delivery cost	$50,000.00
Curriculum delivery cost (FTE)	$1,973.60
Curriculum development hours	0

If we follow through on this example, the formula reads as follows, as table 6 shows:

(30-day expectation minus 30-day actual performance)
multiplied by
(30-day expectation multiplied by employee cost per minute)
finally multiplied by
(30-day actual call volume)
Handle time deviation $= ((5.5 - 6.5) \times (5.5 \times 0.225)) \times (686)$

It is possible to follow through with the deviation calculations for the other metrics or drivers in table 5. You can then add together all of the deviations, and compute your ROI against total training

Table 4. Posttraining performance.

Posttrain Ramp Metrics, 30 Days	Performance Expectation	Current Period
Occupancy	65	63
Call volume	630-850	686
Handle time	5.5	5.6
Abandon rate	5	5
After call work	2.2	2.19
Quality score	84	86
Page views	1,890-2,550	1,979
Work hours (average)	62	64
One call resolution %	10	8.4

Table 5. Posttraining ROI calculation.

ROI Calculation	Current Period
Training delivery cost	$1,973.60
Handle time deviation	$(84.89)
Abandon revenue	$-
After call revenue	$1.54
Page view deviation	$(0.89)
Work hours	$27.00
One call resolution revenue	$(96.94)
ROI calculation	−8%

Table 6. Handle time deviation.

Posttrain ramp metrics, 30 days	Performance Expectation	Current Period
Handle time	5.5	6.5
Call volume	630-850	686
Cost per FTE (minutes)		$0.225
Handle time deviation		$(848.93)

delivery cost. So, the final ROI calculation from table 5 should be equal to the sum of all performance deviations divided by total training delivery costs.

You can repeat the preceding steps for 60 days and 90 days, respectively. Once you have completed those steps, you can then sum up the experience for center one.

Table 7 assembles the final results. Note that the cost of training remains flat. If this fluctuates, insert the actual numbers. Training delivery cost is referenced from table 5, where we calculated the total training delivery cost and divided it among all employees trained.

It is now possible to assemble a graph for center one that shows the results as follows, as shown in figure 4.

The methodology will be identical to get the results for centers two and three. After that, we can proceed to piecing the big picture together, which ties all three centers into one model.

Step Two: Compile the Results for All Three Centers

The final step is to assemble a model that includes all three centers. You already have indicators, or ROI, for each individual location. The next step is to look at the training program as a whole. The model, when complete, should look like table 8.

Now that you've seen the entire call center "roll-up" model, in table 8, I will break the model into individual pieces, as shown in table 9.

Table 9 captures general information about the training that was delivered in each center. Once the model is complete, it proves interesting to adjust these numbers and see its impact on the results. The three items in italics—attrition, job abandon, and curriculum

Table 7. Summary of performance.

Time	30 days	60 days	90 Days
TCPF	$1,973.60	$1,973.60	$1,973.60
TDD	$(154.18)	$284.84	$322.42
CE	−8%	14%	16%

Note:
TCPF, total cost per full-time employee: Identify total cost of training, divided by number of employees trained.
TDD, Identify total deviation per identified driver, then total deviation.
CE, cost-effectiveness: Finalize cost effectiveness calculation, CE = TDD/TCPF.

Figure 4. The ROI results over ramp time.

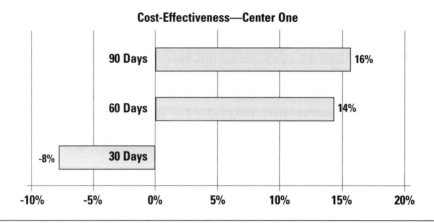

Cost-Effectiveness—Center One

attrition—are optional. In this specific situation, we wanted these numbers included for further comparison among the centers.

Table 10 captures the key financials, by center, for training delivery. Miscellaneous implementation costs can refer to food, toys or prizes, or any other nonessential cost.

In table 11 we annualize the performance results, in dollars, based on the figures from each center. We are making an assumption that the results for 90-day posttraining results remain flat for the rest of the year.

Table 12 shows the measurement of the actual results. Using the figures from table 11, we simply divide the total savings for 12 months by the total training costs. It will show for every dollar spent that we receive "x" dollars in cost savings based on performance. The table shows that for every dollar spent on training, we receive a return of $4.61, or 461 percent, in terms of cost savings. You can compare each center or look at a national (or company) average.

In table 13, we utilize our results to identify opportunity, our what-if scenarios based on the results from the model. In scenario one from table 13, we have $3 million dollars being spent on training, and we are seeing an ROI of 461 percent. Our cost savings equate to approximately $11 million. In scenario two from table 13, we add $500,000 to training, but receive an increased return of almost $2 million.

Scenario three from table 13 again shows the actual results. Scenario four, however, shows an increased ROI of 561 percent. The assumption to draw from this scenario is that increased training effectiveness (100 percent more ROI) would give us an increased cost savings of $3 million. By simply using your results and plugging in

Table 8. ROI summary for all centers.

Class Statistics	Center 1	Center 2	Center 3
Total employees per class	18	15	20
Total training hours per class	162.5	162.5	162.5
Total training hours per FTE	162.5	162.5	162.5
Attrition rate	*	*	*
Job abandon rate	*	*	*
Curriculum attrition	*	*	*

Training Cost	Center 1	Center 2	Center 3	National Average
FTE (rep) cost per minute	$0.24	$0.24	$0.24	$0.24
Design and development cost	$10,880.00	$10,880.00	$10,880.00	$10,880.00
Trainer cost per hour	$24.50	$24.50	$24.50	$24.50
Total trainer cost	$3,981.25	$3,981.25	$3,981.25	$3,981.25
Miscellaneous implementation cost	$500.00	$500.00	$500.00	$500.00
Total training cost	**$15,361.25**	**$15,361.25**	**$15,361.25**	**$15,361.25**

Total Savings over 12 months	Center 1	Center 2	Center 3	National Average
Talk time deviation	$23,397.24	$38,835.72	$6,909.62	$23,047.53
Hold time deviation	$23,116.11	$22,679.08	$14,966.16	$20,253.78
After call work deviation	$11,898.24	$7,372.96	$9,805.55	$9,692.25
Handle time deviation	$56,383.20	$49,278.84	$(52,382.47)	$17,759.86
Total savings	**$114,794.79**	**$118,166.61**	**$(20,701.14)**	**$70,753.42**

Return-on-Investment (ROI)	Center 1	Center 2	Center 3	National Average
Total savings over 12-month period	$114,794.79	$118.166.61	$(20,701.14)	$70,753.42
Total training costs	$15,361.25	$15,361.25	$15,361.25	$15,361.25
Cost saving as a ratio of expense (ROI)	**$7.47**	**$7.69**	**$(1.35)**	**$4.61**

Sensitivity Analysis	Training Budget	ROI %	Cost Savings
Scenario 1	$3,000,000	461	$10,830,000
Scenario 2	$3,500,000	461	$12,635,000
Difference	$500,000	—	$1,805,000
Scenario 3	$3,000,000	461	$10,830,000
Scenario 4	$3,000,000	561	$13,830,000
Difference	$0	100	$3,000,000

* Not applicable. These are optional fields.

Table 9. Statistics by center.

Class Statistics	Center 1	Center 2	Center 3
Total employees per class	18	15	20
Total training hours per class	162.5	162.5	162.5
Total training hours per FTE	162.5	162.5	162.5
Attrition rate	*	*	*
Job abandon rate	*	*	*
Curriculum attrition	*	*	*

* Not applicable. These are optional fields.

Table 10. Training costs by center.

Training Cost	Center 1	Center 2	Center 3	National Average
FTE (rep) cost per minute	$0.24	$0.24	$0.24	$0.24
Design and development cost	$10,880.00	$10,880.00	$10,880.00	$10,880.00
Trainer cost per hour	$24.50	$24.50	$24.50	$24.50
Total trainer cost	$3,981.25	$3,981.25	$3,981.25	$3,981.25
Miscellaneous implementation cost	$500.00	$500.00	$500.00	$500.00
Total training cost	**$15,361.25**	**$15,361.25**	**$15,361.25**	**$15,361.25**

Table 11. Annualization of performance results.

Total Savings Over 12 Months	Center 1	Center 2	Center 3	National Average
Talk time deviation	$23,397.24	$38,835.72	$6,909.62	$23,047.53
Hold time deviation	$23,116.11	$22,679.08	$14,966.16	$20,253.78
After call work deviation	$11,898.24	$7,372.96	$9,805.55	$9,692.25
Handle time deviation	$56,383.20	$49,278.84	$(52,382.47)	$17,759.86
Total savings	**$114,794.79**	**$118,166.61**	**$(20,701.14)**	**$70,753.42**

Table 12. Return-on-investment.

Return-on-Investment (ROI)	Center 1	Center 2	Center 3	National Average
Total savings over 12-month period	$114,794.79	$118,166.61	$(20,701.14)	$70,753.42
Total training costs	$15,361.25	$15,361.25	$15,361.25	$15,361.25
Cost saving as a ratio of expense (ROI)	**$7.47**	**$7.69**	**$(1.35)**	**$4.61**

Table 13. Sensitivity analysis.

Sensitivity Analysis	Training Budget	ROI %	Cost Savings
Scenario 1	$3,000,000	461	$10,830,000
Scenario 2	$3,500,000	461	$12,635,000
Difference	$500,000	-	$1,805,000
Scenario 3	$3,000,000	461	$10,830,000
Scenario 4	$3,000,000	561	$13,830,000
Difference	$0	100	$3,000,000

different budgets and ROI, you can generate a clear picture of what extra money, or efficiency, will return.

This model is adaptable to different organizations. Just keep the methodology simple. All that is necessary is the expectation, the deviation, the associated costs, and training costs.

Costs

The costs for implementing this kind of metric depends largely on an organization's existing resources. My company has ACD systems, IVR systems, and large-scale telephony systems in place. Companies that do not have these systems will find it very costly to implement these metrics. Most of the cost incurred by my group was development time to deliver the model. Once in production, there was almost no cost except for the human resources to pull the data and compile the results.

Results

An executive who looks at the dollar figures of savings may, in some cases, have serious questions about where that money is going. It is a broad statement to say, "We're saving seven dollars for every dollar you spend on training." It is possible to alleviate much confusion by presenting the results of the model with the right disclaimer.

My answer to this problem was to use the ratio in the model, shown in table 13, for comparison purposes only. The final number (or ratio) is still somewhat diluted with cultural influences, call center environment, and the basic skill level of the employees. The statement "Call center one has a ratio of seven to one, while call center two is running at five to one" draws valid conclusions but avoids the finance pitfall. The conclusions appear in figure 5.

The presentation of the results in this fashion makes it possible to draw valid conclusions about the training by center and nationally. It is also possible to identify individual training issues or center hiring issues.

Questions for Discussion

1. How do you modify the model to include customer satisfaction results?
2. How many iterations of the model must be completed before an accurate trend can be delivered?
3. How can the model be adapted to measure curriculum success?
4. How can this model be utilized in forecasting call center performance?
5. How can this model be used to facilitate budgeting in a corporate call center?

The Author

Michael Voellinger is senior manager of operations at a company that asked not to be identified. He has worked in the consumer wireless industry since 1995, with a progressive history involving data warehousing, metrics development, call center operations, performance analysis, budgeting, financial analysis, and systems development. His formal

Figure 5. ROI sampling for comparative results of three centers.

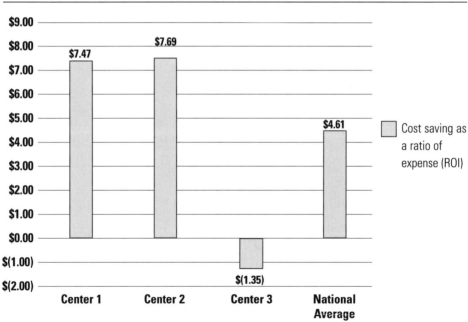

education came from attending St. Thomas Aquinas College in New York, majoring in computer science with a minor in economics. Prior to the wireless industry, he was engaged in the retail industry in both management and information technology capacities. He was the recipient of multiple quality awards within his organization, and was also nominated seven times for his company's national excellence program. He can be reached at his email address mv_essp@yahoo.com.

Training to Focus on Top Accounts to Increase Sales

Trans American Airways

Rich McLafferty

This case study describes a unique approach to call center creation and development, and shows how a nontraditional approach can pay off in customer satisfaction. Through the use of innovative recruiting and training methods as well as motivation techniques, it is possible to maintain a high level of employee satisfaction while doing work that is normally thought of as monotonous and routine. The result is a customer-focused service organization that has earned the reputation of being the best in the industry.

Organizational Profile

Trans American Airways is one of the largest airlines in the United States. The company employs approximately 75,000 employees, and is headquartered in New York City. Trans American Airways is predominately an East Coast carrier with hubs in New York, Washington, D.C., and Boston, Massachusetts. The company has struggled through the years to maintain profitability, mainly due to competitive pricing, a high cost structure, and a challenging route system throughout the eastern corridor.

The company was reorganized in 1996 bringing about changes in upper management, as well as a name and image change from Trans Eastern Airways to Trans American Airways. The carrier was transforming itself from a midsize regional airline into a global carrier with an expansion into major international destinations. These changes required a drastic new approach to sales and to sales support.

This case was prepared to serve as a basis for discussion rather than to illustrate either effective or ineffective administrative and management practices. Names of places, organizations, or people have been disguised at the request of the author or organization.

Industry Profile

The airline industry is extremely competitive, and it generally competes by the price of a ticket. Aircraft look the same, seats are fairly standard, and the basic service is to get from point A to point B safely and on time.

Throughout the 1960s and 1970s, airlines such as Pan Am, Braniff, and Eastern ruled the skies. The government controlled the industry through the Civil Aeronautics Board (CAB). From routes to ticket prices, the CAB kept fares high and eliminated competition. An airline could not fly an airplane commercially on any route without approval from the CAB.

In 1978, President Carter signed the Airline Deregulation Act into law. This allowed each airline to establish individual fare structures and compete on any domestic route. Deregulation caught the airline industry off guard. Many companies were not prepared to run their top-heavy (cost-prohibitive) organizations in this open market environment. Major carriers struggled to remain profitable, and several airlines including Pan Am, Eastern, and Braniff went bankrupt.

Deregulation gave birth to the concepts of frequent flyer programs and to the airport hub and spoke system, and it led to the creation of many new companies, such as People Express. These new carriers increased competition by providing a similar service at a much lower cost (the new entrant carriers had much lower cost structures, labor and operating costs, and were able to pass that savings on to the consumer).

The industry continues to face many challenges. Labor unions representing work groups such as pilots, flight attendants, and mechanics fight for contracts that take many years to negotiate, and sometimes end up in labor disputes. Crowded airports and airplanes put stress on the overall infrastructure; weather delays and cancellations as well as an antiquated air traffic control system can cause massive backups that reek havoc with an airline's operation, and ultimately its bottom line.

These challenges have resulted in increased customer dissatisfaction and enough media attention that politicians in Washington, D.C., have stepped in to facilitate a solution. The government has threatened to introduce legislation in the form of a Passenger Bill of Rights if the industry does not fix the situation on its own. These "rights" would regulate how airlines handle lengthy delays, pricing, lost bags, and a host of other customer complaints. In response, the airlines created their own individual written service agreements and promises on how they will handle a list of operational challenges. Congress is keeping a close watch and is prepared to pass legislation if the situation does not improve.

Background

For many years, Trans American Airways did not face much competition on most of the routes it served. In many markets, Trans American Airways was the only carrier offering service. This led to a very passive sales culture in which account managers did not have to really "sell" due to the lack of competition. Accounts (that is, travel agency and corporate travel departments) basically had to put up with the current level of service because they had no other choice; that was about to change.

Low-cost carriers began offering service to markets previously dominated by Trans American Airways. The increased competition reduced Trans American Airway's market share and revenue in these markets, and with its higher cost structure, the company had to radically change the way it ran its business.

Reorganization

A management team was brought in to reinvent the way Trans American Airways approached sales. The team was challenged to critique every activity, process, and program in the sales department. Sales support was nonexistent; it was left up to the account managers to handle these types of calls in between their account visits. Accounts that needed assistance were forced to leave voice mail messages and hope that an account manager returned their call. On average, account managers had approximately 300 to 350 accounts each. This lack of service led to upset customers who felt frustrated because they had no other choice in air carriers.

The team decided to remove the support and service side of the business from the account managers so they could concentrate on selling. The sales team was divided into Field Sales (managers who would handle major accounts in a geographic territory usually in and around major U.S. cities) and Inside Sales (a centralized group located at headquarters that would handle midtier and major accounts that were not physically located in the Field Sales geographic territories). In addition, it was decided to create an elite centralized support center that major accounts (those accounts that support and sell Trans American Airways) could call into for their special needs and requests.

The vision was to create a sales support center around the customers' business needs. The major accounts were called upon at the beginning of the project to share their ideas and provide feedback. This was very helpful from a customer buy-in perspective and also in ongoing support as the accounts felt a part—ownership—of the new organization. The accounts were involved in major decisions ranging from the types of services that would be offered through the center to the hours that the center would be open.

Initial Design Phase

During the initial design phase, a design team conducted on-site account visits to learn more about the customers' operational needs. The design team spent time with an account's front-line staff learning about its business and how the staff uses competitive services, what the staff members liked, and what they would change. Competitive information was explored in an effort to create the perfect center in the eyes of the customer. The time spent visiting accounts was important to the center's success.

Call Center Design

The center started out with 28 seats and has grown to 54 seats over a two-year period. The center is open from 8 a.m. to 8 p.m. eastern time, and handles calls from corporate travel accounts and travel agency accounts. Top-producing accounts (in excess of $5 million in annual revenue) are the only ones that have access to the call center.

A marketing team was brought in to design a name, logo, and collateral material for the center. The marketing group named the center One Call, and the collateral material included photos of the center and the original class of 28 support managers. The inclusion of the photos of the actual support managers created a true sense of ownership and pride. The collateral was mailed out to the accounts prior to the opening, and it included all of the information they needed to use the new service.

The Grand Opening

Since everything and everyone was new, the center phased in the accounts by geographic location during a soft opening to allow the new support managers to ramp up their skills. This helped them to gain confidence, feel successful, and effectively handle the increasing call volume.

The center management team was in hourly contact with the accounts to get their feedback during the ramp-up period. The accounts' immediate feedback was essential in our ability to identify gaps in training or design, or both, and make corrections as needed. The accounts initial feedback was that it was obvious the group was new (it took longer to complete the transactions, and call times were high in the beginning), "but, boy, were the support managers nice." This feedback supported our philosophy that customers will put up with a lot (as we knew they would have to with a brand new center and service) as long as they are being treated well. The philosophy also proved correct in that the accounts would be understanding and very helpful during the startup period, as long as they knew we were listening and responding to their concerns.

As of the summer of 2001, the center handled approximately 2,500 travel agency and corporate travel department accounts throughout the United States, answering approximately 3,000 inbound calls per day. This represents a 50 percent increase in calls in a three-year period.

Center Technology

An automatic call distribution (ACD) system is used to route calls to the appropriate area (corporate or agency) when the account enters a unique industry identifier. The ACD is programmed to allow access to authorized accounts and to automatically transfer unauthorized accounts to the reservations department. The support managers are "gated" to handle either corporate or agency calls.

The center purposefully avoided using an interactive voice response (IVR) system because it did not want its top accounts to have to choose from endless menu selections. The idea is to make the experience as simple for the customer as possible.

Workstations are modularized in groups of four, with PCs that run both Windows-based programs and an airline reservation system. Monitors and reader boards throughout the center keep everyone updated on number of calls in queue and the average customer waiting time.

Center Development Highlights

The project began in March 1998, and the center opened on time and under budget on June 1, 1998. In that short amount of time the following was accomplished:

- Thirty-five people were recruited, placed, and trained.
- A complete technical and soft skills curriculum was developed.
- An infrastructure was developed including a complete floor build-out; and furniture, equipment, telephone, computer, and ACD installation.
- A complete marketing and advertising campaign was developed and implemented.
- A database of 25,000 customer profiles was created and linked to the ACD.

Recruiting

Recruiting Philosophy

The central recruiting philosophy is, "You can teach people the technical skills in training, but you can't teach them how to be nice." People are selected for their innate people skills, not their technical skills (if they happen to have both, that's an added bonus). The philosophy has paid off over and over again through the positive feedback received from the customers regarding the center's outstanding people.

Four golden rules are followed:

- Treat each candidate as you would treat your best customer: No matter what happens in the end, he or she is either a current or possibly future customer. You don't want him or her leaving with a negative impression of the company or the department.
- Make each candidate feel at ease: The interview process should be fun and enjoyable, not formal and uptight.
- Treat everyone with dignity and respect. Candidates have taken valuable time to participate in the interview: Recognize this and thank each one for his or her time and consideration.
- Look for people (that is, interpersonal) skills first and foremost. Everything else can be developed.

The Interview Process

Recruiting is a three-step process:

- a 1 1/2-hour group information session and interview with eight candidates and two recruiters
- a 15-minute familiarization session and a side-by-side observation session with a support manager in the call center
- a 30-minute one-on-one interview.

INFORMATION SESSION AND GROUP INTERVIEW. The group interview is an in-depth information session about the company, department, and position. Recruiters paint a painfully realistic picture of a typical day and the challenges of call center work. The result of this process is that people come into the job with no surprises. They understand the type of work that is required, which has led to higher job satisfaction and low attrition. The group interview lasts for approximately one and a half hours.

Following the information session, the candidates receive a sheet of 10 questions. The recruiters ask them to take about 10 minutes to select and prepare four questions they would like to answer. The questions are:

1. Tell us about a time when you went beyond the call of duty for a customer.

2. What is your personal definition of outstanding customer service?
3. What is the best example of customer service that you have personally experienced?
4. Tell us about a time when you really felt under pressure.
5. Tell us how you stay motivated at work. What motivates you?
6. If you were teaching a class in customer service, what topics would you include?
7. What are the things the bother you most about people?
8. What skills do you feel are most important to be successful in customer service?
9. You just won a $50 million lottery. How would you spend your time?
10. How are you unique?

The candidates take turns answering the questions until everyone answers four questions. This session gives the recruiters the opportunity to concentrate on both the candidates' responses and their interaction within the group. The recruiters watch for candidates who pay attention and interact with the group. They are looking specifically for interpersonal and listening skills.

CALL CENTER FAMILIARIZATION. Following the group interview, candidates are given a tour of the call center, and then individually participate in a side-by-side observation session with an experienced support manager. The support manager gives a quick overview of the hardware and software, provides his or her personal impression of the job, and answers any questions. The support manager takes a few calls so that candidates get a real-world view of the type of work that they will be expected to do every day. The support managers observe the candidates and provide feedback for the recruiters. Everyone has to work together, so everyone should participate in the selection process.

THE FINAL INTERVIEW. The final interview is a 30-minute session at which recruiters meet with candidates individually and ask behavioral types of questions. The recruiters probe for customer focus, empathy, listening, and motivation to work in a call center environment. The recruiters also look for candidates who view this position as the first step in a career with Trans American Airways.

Retention

Retention during the first year of operation was 100 percent, and today it remains at 97 percent. Career development and career paths were built into the design from the beginning, and they are an important part of employee satisfaction. Most career paths lead to opportunities in sales, training and development, and call center management. The support manager position provides the basic skills and knowledge that are needed to have a successful career in the airline industry.

Support managers are also involved in account management activities, and they participate in joint calls with account managers and in promotional events. This broader involvement breaks the routine of taking endless calls and helps develop the support managers for other positions in the sales department. The account management activities also create a sense of account ownership. Support managers are able to build relationships with the accounts, which is essential for employee and customer satisfaction.

Recruiting is a challenge these days. Positions are continuously posted on the company Website and at university career centers. College and university campus recruiting is also used for both full-time and summer intern positions.

Training
Initial Training Program

Initial training is a comprehensive four-week program that covers both technical and soft skills. The program is interactive and uses classroom (lecture and skill practice) and computer lab (technical skill practice and assessment).

A unique aspect of the program is a module on leadership and systems thinking as it applies to customer service. Trainees study these two areas in an effort to better prepare themselves for their roles as support managers.

The goal is to provide a basic understanding of systems; to view the whole, not look at their job or function as linear. It is also important to understand the concepts of leadership. Taking a leadership position in customer service requires people who are willing to put themselves out there, take risks, and think differently. Support managers are encouraged to view themselves as leaders in customer service. They want to set the standard for the industry, and that differentiates them from the competition. The entire program is taught in the context of leadership and systems thinking.

Technical job-related tasks and skills are taught in knowledge blocks. Knowledge blocks are sets of calls of a certain type (such as fare requests, seat assignments, and special handling requests). Trainees learn how to handle each type of call and the related tasks. The technical modules are hands-on, and the computer system allows trainees to work in a real-time trainee mode. The system simulates the exact environment that the trainees will work in on the job.

Trainees complete sets of knowledge blocks in the classroom, as figure 1 shows, and then go out to the floor with a trainer to apply the knowledge on live calls. A group debriefing for each knowledge block is conducted in the classroom to discuss any challenges and to reinforce learning.

Each call has three components: technical, system, and customer service. The three components as they relate to an individual call create a task. Each task is the integration of one or more technical skills, one or more system skills, and customer service skills. The call-based design helps trainees understand all of the components (tasks) necessary to handle each call they will be required to handle on the job, which results in increased comprehension and productivity (table 1).

Additional reinforcement soft skills modules consist of the following topics:
- consultative customer service skills
- listening and hearing exercises
- telephone etiquette and skills
- decision making
- challenging customers
- stress management
- balance in the workplace and finding your passion.

Figure 1. Diagram of curriculum design.

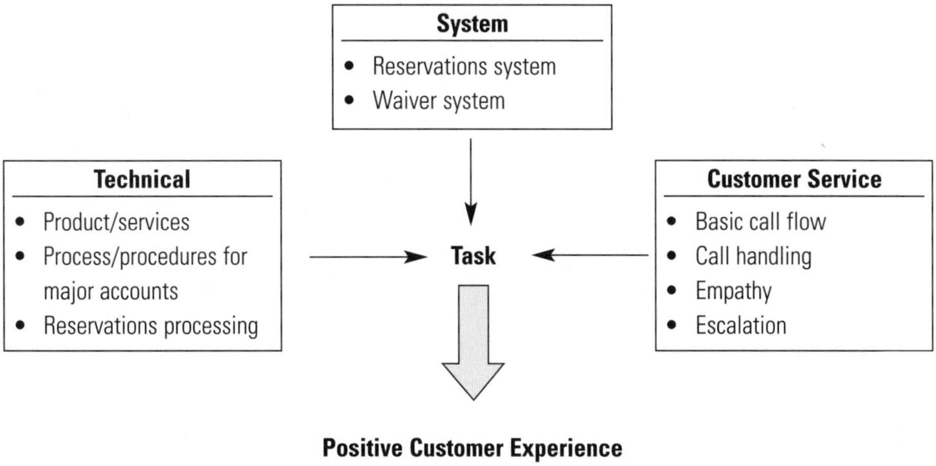

System
- Reservations system
- Waiver system

Technical
- Product/services
- Process/procedures for major accounts
- Reservations processing

Task

Customer Service
- Basic call flow
- Call handling
- Empathy
- Escalation

Positive Customer Experience

Table 1. Comparison matrix.

Systems-Based Training	Task-Based Training
Compatible only in a generalist (market) environment	Compatible with generalist or specialist environments (skill-based routing)
Leaves integration of content in the hands of the learner	Fully integrated content to allow for practice and mastery of skills
Measures success by ability to recall knowledge, not apply knowledge	Provides greater validity through instructional approach that mirrors the job
Learners' ability to ramp up to full potential is limited by their ability to effectively learn the job as they go	Decreases ramp up by promoting skills, knowledge, and ability transfer from training to the job

Assessments

Another unique concept of the training program is self-assessment. Trainees are given self-assessments throughout the program. Each trainee maintains a running average of his or her assessments, and together with the instructor determines areas for improvement or additional development. Success in the program is a team effort between trainees and instructor. Trainees are given the responsibility to assess and continuously monitor their level of achievement and to seek out assistance when necessary.

Call centers tend to create environments that do not allow people to think on their own. They are places in which every minute of a representative's time is accounted for and monitored. The One Call program attempts to give trainees a feeling of control and ownership and to foster a mindset of responsibility for their own learning and their ultimate success.

Treat people like adults, and you get adult behavior; treat them like children, and you get less than what you hope for. The support managers learn why it is important to be on the phones and the business reasons for maintaining high levels of customer satisfaction. The result at One Call is that we do not need to monitor the floor for occupancy. The team takes responsibility for maintaining a high-service level, and it will reschedule breaks and lunch periods if necessary. This team environment is a major reason for such high customer satisfaction.

It has also helped the center create an environment of continuous learning. When people take responsibility for their success, they tend to seek out knowledge and skills that help them become better at what they do. This method also takes into consideration each person's own unique styles of learning and assessment, and it better prepares them to make sound business decisions when on the job.

Recurrent training as well as continuing education is available for those seeking additional assistance once on the job and for those who promote into supervisory and management positions in the center. There is also a Walk-a-Mile program to encourage the support managers to learn about their sales and service colleagues' jobs and to also explore future career opportunities.

Additional development opportunities are identified through remote and side-by-side monitoring. Supervisors are required to monitor their teams at least twice a month, following up with immediate feedback and coaching sessions.

The Business Results

Customers continue to be pleased with the new organization and service, and sales have increased by significant amounts. The airline's image has also changed dramatically. Accounts no longer feel that they are not supported, or appreciated.

It is difficult to quantify sales results directly related to the call center. Many factors, such as a new sales organization, new sales programs, and new training and development programs, played a part in the overall change in customer satisfaction and increased sales.

The sales and service group is encouraged to act as one; a seamless and consistent experience where the sales team members work with their support team counterparts to ensure customer satisfaction.

A Note about Service

Three months following the grand opening, the team started conducting official customer satisfaction surveys. Since that time the average score has been at 98 percent as "extremely satisfied." An interesting note about customer satisfaction: A mistake was made with a database allowing a large amount of additional accounts access to the center. There was a significant spike in inbound calls, without any additional resource, which increased customer wait times to approximately 20 minutes. Even during this time, customer satisfaction surveys remained at 98 percent, indicating it must have been worth the wait!

Happy Landings

Today, the center is still viewed as the true success story that resulted from the massive reorganization, especially in the customers' eyes. They thought it could not be done, but now share in the success.

The customers still are involved today. They attend open houses at the center, host luncheons for the support managers, send gifts, and participate in the training programs to educate the group about their business and their unique needs.

Lessons Learned

Following are some of the lessons Trans American Airways learned from implementation of its revamped call center:

- Get the customer involved as much as you can in the beginning, and keep the customer involved. Customer involvement truly builds a concrete relationship that allows for candid and constructive communication. Problems and situations can be handled in a much faster and efficient manner, before they turn into a crisis. Customer involvement has helped minimize needless fire-fighting, allowing for a much more positive and productive environment.

- "Hire the athletes, and train them in the game." Hire customer contact people for "people" skills. You can teach them the rest, but you cannot teach them how to be nice.

- Make people responsible for their own success. Start the process in training and keep the philosophy alive throughout their career. Call centers tend to foster dependent types of behaviors. Keep people engaged and focused through continual feedback and coaching. Make them feel like an integral part of the business. Front-line people can make or break a company.

- Teach them about the whole business. That is the only way that they can make sound business decisions and know when to ask the important questions.

- Do not try to teach people to be experts in everything; you are wasting your time. Teach them how to locate the resources required to handle the calls. That helps foster an environment of continual learning.

- Constantly push career development. In call center work there is going to be turnover. People burn out, but they do not lose the institutional knowledge. Create career paths that take that knowledge to higher levels, and build on the depth and breadth of the overall organization.

- Have fun. Do not take it all so seriously. Call center work is draining for everyone involved. If the people on the phones are not enjoying themselves, then the customer is not having a positive experience either. Do crazy fun things that break the pressure and monotony. That keeps the call center energized, alive, and positive.

Questions for Discussion

1. What was the purpose of the initial design phase?
2. How did the activities in this affect the outcome of the project?
3. What were the four basic rules in the recruiting process?
4. Did the new recruiting mindset work by recruiting nice people? Why?
5. Why did it make a difference that they asked their customers what they wanted?
6. Why did the training program change employees' attitudes?

The Author

Rich McLafferty is the West Coast regional manager for vendor relations at a major telecommunications company. He has held numerous positions, including training and development, sales and marketing, and organizational development projects for several major U.S. airlines including Pan Am, American Airlines, and US Airways. He holds a bachelor's degree in humanities and a master's degree in organizational development. His work and research interests are in creating more people-centered—humane, inclusive, and collaborative—work environments. He can be reached at rmclafferty@earthlink.net.

Experiential Learning Via Call Simulations to Improve Customer Service

A Data and Voice Communication Service Company

Michelle Lavoie

A primary objective of many call centers is a reduction in customer care representatives' time to achieve competency. New representatives often are subject to a three- to six-month learning curve that is directly related to the complexity of the customer support they deliver. During this period they are, in effect, practicing on customers. While their enthusiasm is often remarkable, their ability to provide accurate and complete information, to achieve call quality metrics, and to achieve call management objectives is often affected by their lack of experience.

This case study describes a customer care simulation model that gets employees up to speed quickly by requiring students to translate their new product and service knowledge into demonstrable skills in a simulated work environment.

Customer Relationship Summary: Reactive Versus Proactive Contact

In general, customer service tends to focus on responding to customer inquiries about billing or service availability. Organizations staff call centers with hundreds of customer service representatives who wait for customer calls and manage them. Representatives are measured on hold times, average handle times, customer satisfaction, and other data-driven metrics. At its core, customer service is reactive and is designed to satisfy a particular customer's issue or need. Customer

This case was prepared to serve as a basis for discussion rather than to illustrate either effective or ineffective administrative and management practices. Names of places, organizations, or people have been disguised at the request of the author or organization.

expectations, however, have changed with growing competition and the increasing globalization of technology and information.

No longer is *customer service* the mantra, but rather *customer care*. Customer care implies a new relationship with customers, a relationship driven by proactive communication and proactive solutions. No longer can call centers wait for a customer to contact them with a question or issue; as customer care providers, call centers must initiate contact to offer new services, to alert customers to potential service interruptions, or in general to provide a high-touch, personalized relationship.

An example of proactive customer care is demonstrated by a data and voice communication service company's response when it experiences system interruptions. This company alerts customers to potential service outages and provides hourly status updates with anticipated resolution times. Customers respond to these announcements not with disappointment, but with gratitude that the company values the relationship enough to notify them. This example demonstrates how customer care transcends the boundaries of traditional service by developing a partnering relationship.

In this highly competitive environment, the ability to provide a high-touch experience is a critical customer care differentiator. There are many benefits to call centers that implement learning practices that yield world-class customer care representatives. Retaining talented, skilled employees is a high priority so companies can benefit by increasing employee retention. Customers benefit by securing service that meets, and exceeds, their high expectations. Employees benefit by developing new skills that they can easily apply in the work environment. While this case details the use of customer call simulations as a learning tool, the concept can be easily applied to customer care that is delivered over the Web or via other communications mediums.

Learning organizations face unique challenges when preparing employees for this new customer care role. Call centers routinely provide learning experiences that emphasize product or service knowledge, relying on knowledge measures or other types of testing to validate learning. A strategically focused curriculum emphasizing customer relationship building is critical to the delivery of memorable customer care. A proactive call center provides high-touch care that requires specialized recruiting and training for call center agents. This case study will introduce the customer call simulation process as one learning methodology that has supported the delivery of world-class customer care.

Overview

Many companies devote a great deal of time to developing knowledge-based curricula. For example, a local technical support provider provides five weeks of highly structured software application training. Employees are taught hundreds, and often thousands, of features associated with particular software or applications products. Employees require this extensive knowledge base since they provide technical support to end users, but other key customer care skills are noticeably absent from the learning cycle.

A comprehensive customer care training program necessarily involves the delivery of industry specific knowledge, including knowledge of
- products or services
- internal processes and procedures
- required interactions with other functional areas
- customer care or quality standards.

Effective training of customer care professionals, though, requires a holistic approach that emphasizes the delivery and assessment of both knowledge and skill. Keeping in mind that a critical goal is to reduce employees' time to competency (that is, reduced time to meet all performance metrics including customer satisfaction), we must deliberately structure learning experiences to include multiple opportunities for skill practice, development, and demonstration.

The data and voice communication service company described in this document initiated a customer care simulation model that required students to translate their new product and service knowledge into demonstrable skills. Throughout the learning cycle, students were required to manage mock customer calls in a simulated work environment. This simulation model reproduces the real-world job, allows multiple opportunities to achieve customer care standards, and provides a valid measurement of both knowledge and skill.

This document will detail the call simulation model, including:
- model summary including foundational assumptions
- development of minimum customer care standards
- preparation of students for the customer simulation experience
- delivery of effective group feedback

- instructor's role in evaluative feedback of customer simulations
- supervisory and organizational benefits.

Organizational Profile
The Challenge

The company provides bundled data and voice communication services to customers in the Northeast corridor. It had acquired one customer care center in New England that provided Internet and data support. Based on the expanding ability to provide local and long distance telephone services in multiple markets, the company initiated a second customer care center to support voice services. A learning organization, the company had only 45 days to ramp up from 0 to 60 customer care representatives, a challenging goal that provided a unique opportunity to develop, design, and implement effective learning practices.

The Solution: Recruiting via Behavioral Interviewing

The recruiting team, consisting of two full-time HR professionals, relied heavily on Web-centered searches to identify skilled customer care candidates and to minimize recruiting costs. Using a behavioral interviewing approach, the team asked each candidate to recount customer care experiences and to detail approaches and outcomes. All candidates had previous service experience that spanned a wide array of environments, ranging from food service work to experience at competing telecommunications providers. The team's focus on customer care skills and competencies enabled us to accurately assess each candidate's ability to provide world-class care.

The Solution: The Right Training Staff

The learning organization faced unique challenges. The director of learning was the only professional with direct responsibility for workplace learning, and few organizational support structures existed. The challenge was to develop a comprehensive curriculum from the ground up, and the goal was to deliver learning that would yield loyal employees and loyal customers. Cognizant of the budget and the challenges that we faced in a full ramp-up of zero to 60 employees in 45 days, the team first identified critical roles and responsibilities associated with the development and delivery of learning.

DESIGNING THE CURRICULUM. The company offers a number of tele-communications and data products to customers. Each of these products is fully documented in a product guide that details technical requirements and capabilities, and describes target markets. Unfor-tunately, the product guide was a marketing brief and not easily transferable to a learning environment. Although the content was solid, the product information was not structured in a format that supported learning.

As a result, the author identified the need for a part-time curriculum designer to translate product guides into a standardized learning format. The curriculum designer's first goal was to design a format for the leaders' and participants' guides that would drive curriculum development going forward. Target audience, learning objectives, content, key discussion questions, learning activities, and learning checks were integrated into the final template to provide trainers and learners with a structured road map for learning.

Each product guide was then translated into a format for the leaders' and participants' guides. This key foundational step set the stage for the development of learning curricula, and the delivery of consistent learning experiences throughout the company.

LEARNING SPECIALIST. The identification of a learning specialist subsequently took precedence as several leaders' guides were under development and customer care staff were in various stages of the hiring process. The learning specialist was primarily responsible for the delivery of learning in the customer care center. While many programs were developed internally, a number were purchased from training providers. Whatever the source, the learning specialist was responsible for using leader materials to effectively and efficiently deliver the knowledge and skills that supported achievement of our corporate goals.

With critical roles identified, the new learning delivery team, which included the author, was faced with the unique challenge of mapping a seven-day new-hire curriculum. Our goal was to deliver qualified customer care professionals to our operation's partners: customer care professionals who not only knew and understood our various service offerings but who also had a demonstrated ability to initiate and develop high-quality relationships with our customers.

Based on past experience, we knew that many customer care centers rely primarily on product or process knowledge to provide learning. For example, a local technical support organization routinely provided customer care representatives with up to five weeks of software knowledge during new-hire training with only minimal attention to customer care delivery skills. The result was a technically proficient customer "service" agent who often experienced difficulty relating to customers in a meaningful way. As the director of learning at the telecommunications provider, my premise was that product or process knowledge does not necessarily equate to customer care skill.

Recognizing the need to integrate skill development with knowledge delivery, our company faced a second challenge: employee retention. Customer care organizations are characterized by turnover rates ranging from 30 percent to 60 percent annually. Recognizing the value of retention, our learning team developed a curriculum that focused on delivering a realistic job preview. This is not an altogether altruistic goal. Employee recruiting and training are significant investments, and new employees' learning curves have a direct impact on customer satisfaction. Preparing new employees for the work environment and developing their ability to accurately and efficiently manage customers clearly benefits the organization, the employee, and customers.

A Balanced Learning Equation: Customer and Employee Loyalty

The learning delivery team's challenge was to construct a balanced learning equation that would yield the required result: customer and employee loyalty. Maintaining our existing customer base was intrinsically tied to maintaining our employee base. Our effort focused on developing a curriculum that would integrate knowledge delivery with demonstrated customer care skills.

Make Versus Buy

The learning organization purchased segments of our customer care curriculum to maximize our ability to target curriculum development to those areas that were company-specific. Listening, problem resolution, effective questioning, and communication skills all existed in established learning curricula purchased from training providers, enabling our curriculum designer to continue developing customized product and service curricula.

Technical and Customer Service Skill Training

With the learning pieces in place, we considered our first goal: retaining employees. Experience suggested that many customer care representatives voluntarily leave their positions within the first few months of employment due to unrealistic job expectations. A job candidates' knowledge that he or she will be in a cube for eight hours a day speaking with customers who are sometimes unhappy is cerebral, whereas sitting in a cube for eight hours a day, speaking with customers who are sometimes unhappy is experiential. Knowledge of the work environment delivered during prehire screening is a poor substitute for a simulated work experience.

Retaining customers is a parallel goal. Customers expect, and often demand, a highly skilled customer care representative who is able not only to provide technical or informational resolutions, but also to initiate a partnering relationship. In the traditional classroom environment, new employees are provided with the technical knowledge to effectively resolve a customer's issue. Opportunities to translate that knowledge into a demonstrable skill are often lacking. The curriculum we developed would have to emphasize skills such as empathizing, negotiating, and partnering, all of which are necessary to the delivery of world-class customer care.

The requirement to retain employees and to retain customers necessarily led the learning delivery team to the initiation of the customer call simulation process. This concept is not revolutionary; in fact, it seems rather intuitive. It is a concept based on the fundamental premise that learners must be exposed to a learning experience that replicates the work environment in every way possible.

STEP ONE: CUSTOMER CALL SIMULATION PROCESS. This step includes identifying quality standards and key behavioral talents.

- *Defining quality standards:* The customer call simulation process assumes that call quality standards have been developed. These standards clearly define exemplary customer care behaviors and provide each employee with detailed performance expectations. Since the company had only recently acquired a customer care center and was in the initial phases of developing requirements for a second customer care center, it did not have generally accepted call quality standards. Many organizations develop these standards in collaboration with customer care center management, but we looked to existing employees as key contributors to this process.

- *Asking employees for key behavioral talents:* Managers were asked to identify star performers on the basis of their ability to calm angry or irate customers, to accurately troubleshoot and resolve customer issues, and to achieve customer care metrics. The director of learning then conducted two focus groups involving 16 star customer care representatives. Each focus group participant was asked, "What do you do or say to provide excellent customer care?" In most cases, participants responded with generalized statements such as "I'm patient" or "I establish a relationship with customers."

The facilitator used directed questions to focus participants on describing behavioral indicators of star performance. As a result, their initial responses were translated into behaviors that were subsequently used to develop the company's call quality standard. A sample of responses from the focus groups and the resulting behaviors elicited by the facilitator is shown in table 1.

The star performers developed a list of key behaviors that yield satisfied customers, spanning a number of different call segments. These included opening the call, identifying the problem, exploring alternatives, recommending solutions, documenting the case, and closing the call. Each of these behaviors was incorporated into a call quality standard, shown in figure 1, providing the basis for the customer call simulation process.

STEP TWO: CUSTOMER CALL SIMULATIONS. This step sets employee expectations. Upon hire, each customer care professional is advised that he or she will be an active participant in a seven-day learning experience that will include classroom learning and customer call simulations. Expectations are set prehire and are reinforced during the initial few hours of training. While many learners initially express discomfort with call simulations, the learning specialist emphasizes the safety of the learning environment and the value of practicing new skills in the classroom.

Customer call simulations are best introduced early in the learning experience, preferably on the morning of day two during a seven-day training cycle. By that time, students have been exposed

Table 1. Behavioral talents.

Star Performer Initial Responses	Behavioral Indicators
I'm patient.	I let the customer finish describing his or her problem before I say anything. I explain the issue to the customer a second time, using different words if he or she doesn't understand.
I establish a relationship with the customer.	I use the customer's name throughout the call. I tell the customer that I've experienced the same problem myself.
I care about the customer.	I tell the customer how badly I feel that he or she is having a problem. I call many customers the next day to ensure that their problems are solved.

Figure 1. Call quality standard.

Activity	Not Applicable	Achieved	Not Achieved	Observations
Greet Customer				
State company name				
Give customer care representative's name				
Is this (name on account?)				
May I call you (customer's first name)?				
How may I help you today?				
Acknowledge Request				
I'll be glad to help you with that.				
Restate customer's problem statement.				
Review customer's trouble ticket history.				
Acknowledge previous support calls, if any.				
Express Empathy				
State "I'm sorry that happened."				
Request Permission to Fact Find				
State "Could I ask a few questions about what happened?"				
Ask Relevant Questions				
When was the last time you could...?				
What has changed since that time?				
When did you last restart your computer?				
Call Transfers				
Get full understanding of issue prior to transfer.				
Review queue in technical area.				
Ask if customer is at home and if the computer is turned on.				
Advise approximate wait time; offer callback option.				

(continued on page 136)

Figure 1. Call quality standard (continued).

Activity	Not Applicable	Achieved	Not Achieved	Observations
Problem Solving				
Authenticate the problem FIRST.				
Verify all assumptions with the customer.				
Duplicate the customer's error.				
Placing Customer on Hold				
Request permission to place on hold.				
"I need to gather more information."				
Secure customer's permission to hold.				
Thank customer for holding.				
Provide Accurate, Complete Responses				
If inexperienced, go screen by screen.				
Educate the customer.				
Verify the Solution				
Advise customer to log on and log off immediately.				
Speak with or email customer to verify. (A busy signal does not equal solution verified.)				
"Have I answered your questions today?"				
Follow-up Commitments				
Set date and time for callback. (1 hour callback if 3 calls within 24 hours.)				
Offer Opportunity for Additional Questions				
"Is there something else I can help with?"				
Express Customer's Value				
"Thanks for choosing (company name)."				
Document Conversation				
Describe the customer's issue.				

Activity	Not Applicable	Achieved	Not Achieved	Observations
Detail anything changed, added, or deleted.				
Detail programs reviewed, step by step.				
Document relevant history (storms, etc.?).				
Document callback commitment and outcome.				
Agent Adaptability				
Accurately assesses customer.				
Modifies approach based on customer skill.				
Uses "I" or "we" in place of "you."				
Minimizes pauses, "ums," or "ahs."				
Eliminates jargon with inexperienced customers.				

Summary comments and observations:

to the call quality standard and are able to demonstrate the behaviors associated with opening the call. These typically include identifying the company name and the customer care representative's name and expressing a willingness to help. These simple behaviors provide an opportunity for learners to experience success in a call simulation process, yielding increased comfort as the complexity of customer call simulations increases.

The learning specialist introduces the call simulation process by clearly defining the purpose, process, and payoff of the experience. A sample statement might include:

> Now, we're going to practice opening the call. Each of you will have an opportunity to assume the role of a customer care provider. A "mock" customer will call, and you will open the call using the company's call quality standards. The class will observe and, using the call quality standard, will indicate which behaviors you have demonstrated. Then, each class member will tell you one thing he or she liked about your opening, and one thing that you might do differently next time. When you've completed this

customer call simulation, you will be able to effectively open a call and achieve the company's call opening standard.

This statement sets clear expectations and defines how the simulation will benefit the employee. It also reinforces that achievement of the call quality standard is a critical performance dimension.

STEP THREE: CUSTOMER CALL SIMULATIONS. The interactive practice and familiarity with job expectations, work organization, and customer care delivery yield high-quality service beginning with the first "live" customer. The call simulation process assumes that the work area is replicated in the learning environment. Each learner must have access to a working telephone and to any required reference materials. The goal is to provide a realistic job simulation that accurately mirrors the work experience. This experience provides not only direct customer care practice, but also practice using equipment and resources.

Many customer support organizations have a detailed issue escalation process. It is important to replicate that process during the call simulations. This company had lead customer care representatives who provide technical and customer care support to requesting employees. During the customer call simulations, we assigned an experienced representative to act as a lead. The learner was then able to dial the lead as needed for assistance, providing an opportunity to utilize and practice the escalation process.

The outcome of an effective customer call simulation process can be observed when the employee manages his or her first live customer call. It is not unusual for the new customer care representative to ask, "Is this a real call?" when he or she hears the customer's opening statement. The experience provided during the customer call simulation process is an effective skill builder that provides a solid foundation from which to provide excellent service.

STEP FOUR: CUSTOMER CALL SIMULATIONS. This step involves preparing for the simulation and conducting it.

- *Preparing for the simulation experience.*
  — *Class size:* The customer call simulation process is most effective when conducted in groups of eight to 10 participants. Group size will drive the efficiency of the process and the effectiveness of feedback delivery. Generally speaking, if an average call simulation requires an eight-minute customer interaction, you must allot an additional 10 minutes for feedback delivery (assuming 10 participants providing one minute of feedback each). This scheduling translates into approximately three hours for call simulations conducted with 10 participants.

If your class size is larger than the 10 recommended participants, solicit assistance from customer care managers or experienced customer care representatives. In this situation, it is imperative that each facilitator has both the knowledge and skills required to effectively observe performance and facilitate feedback delivery. If possible, select facilitators in advance of the scheduled call simulations and ask them to participate in, and observe, the process before assuming responsibility for group facilitation.

— *The first simulation:* The first simulation relies heavily on establishing and maintaining a safe and comfortable environment for learners. It should occur early in the learning cycle and should provide an opportunity to successfully demonstrate a fundamental skill. It is recommended that the initial customer call simulation should be opening the call because it is highly likely to result in learner success and set the foundation for future call simulations.

Carefully select the learner for the first simulation experience. Select someone who has been participative and who has a high probability of demonstrating the required skills successfully. If possible, approach the learner before the simulation and ask him or her to participate in the first simulation. Learning is cumulative, and each subsequent participant will build upon the knowledge and skills demonstrated previously so a strong initial performance will yield dividends in individual performance.

— *Opening the call:* It is critical to define successful performance before implementing the customer call simulation process. The first call simulation, opening the call, requires the learner to demonstrate all of the behaviors associated with the following:
  • greeting the customer
  • acknowledging the request
  • expressing empathy.
Since these calls are short in duration, the learner is provided two opportunities if required.

— *Call scenarios:* Carefully consider the placement of subsequent call simulations and develop scenarios that integrate product or service knowledge with a demonstration of call quality standards. First, consider the complexity of the scenario. Following is an example of a call scenario.

Customer information: Your name is Jane Smith, and this is the third time that you call about this problem. You are not happy. You're at work, and your phone is constantly ringing. You can't believe that it's taking three calls to resolve this issue.

Opening statement: My name is Jane Smith, and this is the third time I'm calling about this. I didn't make the long distance call on my bill.

Suggested path: If and when the customer care representative acknowledges that this is your third call and apologizes, assume a friendly and cooperative tone and manner.

Scenarios should be neither too complex nor too simple. To develop scenarios, consult with site management or site employees to identify the 10 most frequent customer issues. Involve experienced customer care professionals or observe customer calls to determine both the content and tone of a typical caller.

Using this information, develop structured scenarios to use during the customer call simulation process. Scenarios should include:
• a brief summary of the customer's state of mind, tone of voice, frequency of calls for assistance, and special circumstances
• the customer's opening statement (verbatim)
• a suggested conversation path.

Each scenario should identify the key behaviors that will most effectively manage the customer. In the sample scenario, key behaviors include acknowledging the customer's frustration and apologizing.

— *The second simulation:* The second simulation, composed of one call, is longer in duration and more complex in nature. As a result, learners are required to demonstrate all of the skills associated with:
• greeting the customer
• acknowledging the request
• expressing empathy
• requesting permission to fact find
• offering opportunity for additional questions
• expressing customer's value.

At this point in the curriculum, learners are not fully prepared to conduct effective troubleshooting or to fully document a customer's issue in the company's case documentation model. The simulation provides an opportunity to develop questioning and problem-solving skills and to benefit from observer feedback.

— *The third simulation:* The third and final series of customer call simulations, with each learner managing two customer issues, fully integrates the customer care process. Using the call quality standard as a guide through the conversation, the learner is required to achieve 25 of the 33 verbal behaviors, or 80 percent, assuming that all apply. The learner must demonstrate compliance with all five of the conversation documentation requirements. If the learner does not achieve these performance standards in the classroom, the learning specialist conducts a one-on-one coaching session and provides the learner with additional opportunities to observe and practice service delivery in the deficient performance dimension. Detailed feedback is provided to the supervisor, who continues the coaching and development process. Figure 2 contains the call simulation performance summary sheet that the learning specialist provides to the supervisor or team leader. This detailed description of the student's performance during the final call simulations provides the team leader with targeted items to observe and fully develop. Although the document is presented here in a paper-based format, it can easily be converted into an automated reporting form by using database creation and management software.

- *Conducting the call simulation.* Another learner, the instructor, or a third party assumes the role of the customer and dials in to the representative. Using the scenario, the customer makes an opening statement and responds to the representative. The customer should be as realistic as possible, providing the learner with reality-based experience that is easily transferable to the job. The representative uses the call quality standard and any associated product or service reference materials to manage the customer's question, issue, or problem. Reference materials or resources available in the workplace should be available in the learning environment to provide a realistic job preview.

  It is important to provide each learner with a copy of the call quality standard. The customer care representative will reference the call quality standard to ensure compliance with the requirements, while each observer will use it to check off the items achieved by the representative during the call simulation. Additionally, observers should document specifically what the representative said or did to demonstrate the behavior. Facilitation may be required during feedback delivery to ensure that observers deliver behavior-based feedback.

  — *Observer feedback:* Following the demonstration, each observer provides feedback including " I really liked the way you . . ." and "Next time, you might want to try. . . ." The facilitator must ensure that feedback is behavior based and comprehensive since most learning participants will tend to make general statements and avoid delivering constructive feedback. Each customer care representative, upon completion of the simulation experience, is provided with documented feedback from each observer (the call quality standard).

Figure 2. Call simulation performance summary.

Customer Care Representative: _____ **Date:** _____

Trainer/Quality/Manager: _____

Performance Summary: Qualify _____ (copy to team leader)
Provisional Release _____ (copy team leader and manager)

	Call 1	Call 2
Greets customer (company name, representative name, express willingness to help)		
Acknowledges customer request (restates problem, reviews trouble tickets)		
Expresses empathy		
Requests permission to fact find		
Asks relevant questions (when was the last time..., what has changed?)		
Transfers calls (gains understanding of issue, reviews queues, ensures customer preparation)		
Solves problems (authenticates problem, verifies assumptions, duplicates the error)		
Places customer on hold (requests permission, provides reason, secures customer's permission, thanks customer for holding upon return)		
Provides accurate and complete responses (educates customer)		
Verifies solutions (confirms solution, asks "Have I answered all your questions?")		
Follows up with customers (sets a date and time for customer commitments)		
Offers opportunity for additional questions		
Expresses customers' value		
Documents the conversation (describes the issue, details what occurred, reviews steps attempted and relevant history, details commitments and/or outcomes)		
Agent's adaptability (assesses customer, modifies approach, uses "we" versus "you" terminology, minimizes pauses, minimizes use of jargon)		

Other Minimum Skills Assessment:

Demonstrated Use of Telephone _____ yes _____ no

Demonstrated Use of PC _____ yes _____ no

Knowledge Measure(s) Scores: _____ % required _____ % achieved

_____ % required _____ % achieved

CALL #1

Strengths:

What I May Have Done Differently:

CALL #2

Strengths:

What I May Have Done Differently:

— *Rotating roles:* Roles are rotated so that each student has an opportunity to assume the role of customer care representative, and each has multiple opportunities to observe and evaluate customer care performance. As the simulations progress, the quality of feedback progressively increases. Observers become more proficient at assessing simulation performance against the call quality standard, increasing their own skill in the process.

— *Subsequent simulations:* Learners often breathe a sigh of relief following the first simulation experience. The initial experience is designed to provide an easily achievable result and to acquaint learners with the process. Subsequent simulations increase in complexity by integrating product or service knowledge with problem resolution skills. Upon completion of three simulation cycles (the last requiring the management of two customer calls) and the balance of the learning curriculum, employees are fully prepared to manage their first live customer.

STEP FIVE: CUSTOMER CALL SIMULATIONS. The fifth step is to assess the outcome. It is difficult to evaluate outcomes because pre- and post-simulation performance data is not available. Of the 60 employees hired while this document was under development, one resigned following the first customer call simulation. This caused significant concern as we considered whether the process was too stressful, or whether we had not prepared our students appropriately for the experience. After extensive discussions with the learning specialist and the employee, our learning delivery team agreed that the inability to manage the stress associated with the call simulation process is predictive of the inability to effectively manage stress in a customer care center environment. In this case, the employee deselected herself from employment, and from the customer care role. Although an unfortunate outcome, our investment in this employee was in fact minimized by the customer call simulation process.

Once representatives were released to the workplace, they frequently referenced their customer call simulation experience. Of all that they learned, they often pointed to the application of knowledge and skill as the best preparation for the uncertainty and stress associated with managing multiple customers and multiple customer issues. A call center representative's ability to provide world-class service is only enhanced by the customer call simulation process.

Conclusions and Recommendations

The customer call simulation process is a natural application of adult learning principles. It provides a realistic job preview and a number of opportunities to translate new product or service knowledge into skilled customer care delivery. It exposes employees to the work environment and bridges the gap between learning and performance. While this discussion has centered primarily on customer care provided by telephone, it can easily be applied to environments with a heavier reliance on the delivery of customer care via email.

Going forward, this process could easily be applied to prehire screening so that companies could accurately assess a job candidate's ability to manage the stresses of customer care delivery. Used in this way, customer call simulations would enhance the employee selection process and provide opportunities for candidate deselection prior to the financial investments inherent in the hiring and training processes.

In existing learning organizations, it is often difficult to redirect learning specialists or instructors to integrate customer call simulations into the learning curriculum. In many cases, they have been selected for a training role on the basis of their technical, product, or service knowledge. As a result, they tend to emphasize the delivery of product or service knowledge in any learning initiative. To overcome instructors' objections, it is important to clearly state that the goal of learning delivery is to develop customer care representatives who are able to demonstrate and deliver care that meets or exceeds company standards and customer expectations. Customer call simulations are natural contributors to employee retention, customer satisfaction, and employee loyalty.

Questions for Discussion

1. What is a call simulation?
2. How can the call simulation process contribute to decreased time to competency?
3. How much experiential training is included in your new-hire curriculum?
4. How does the employee benefit from call simulation training?
5. How does the customer benefit from call simulation training?
6. What would a call simulation process look like in an environment that relies on email communication with customers?

The Author

Michelle Lavoie is a global technical training manager at EMC in Milford, Massachusetts, providers of enterprise information infrastructures. Prior to this position, she was the director of learning at Log On America, a voice and data communications provider, and the senior manager of field learning at Stream International, a premier technical solutions provider. Her past experience includes seven years at A.T. Cross, a manufacturer of fine writing instruments, and seven years at AT&T. Lavoie's diverse background in the technical, telecommunications, and manufacturing industries has provided her with unique opportunities to apply structured processes to a variety of learning initiatives. She can be reached at EMC, 5 Technology Drive, Milford, MA 01757; phone: 508.346.5430; email: lavoie_michelle@emc.com.

Achieving Future State Training

Duke Power

Trina A. Stephens

Duke Power's call center is located in a rapidly growing section of Charlotte, North Carolina, a city that houses at least 12 other established call centers, with several more under construction. Competition for employees among these centers is fierce and has led to high turnover rates in the local market. As a proactive response to the difficulties inherent in obtaining, training, and retaining the best employees, Duke decided to redesign its base training program to better position itself in the current market environment. This case study examines the training redesign process and reveals how Duke Power is using people and processes to achieve its business objectives.

Background

Duke Power, a subsidiary of Duke Energy, provides electric utility services to more than two million customers in North and South Carolina. The almost 100-year-old company seeks to provide, among other things, "reliable electricity at competitive prices." To help accomplish this goal, Duke operates a centralized, customer call center in Charlotte, North Carolina.

The training for new phone specialists at Duke's call center, prior to the redesign, was primarily instructor led. Employees were recruited and hired with the goal of having them start training in groups of about 20 people. In order to fill a class, an employee's first day on the job was often scheduled several weeks after the person was offered a position. During these intervening weeks, many new employees quit to take

This case was prepared to serve as a basis of discussion rather than to illustrate either effective or ineffective administrative and management practices.

jobs with other companies, a situation that created a difficult recruiting and training loop for the Duke staff. The timeframe for Duke to break even on costs associated with recruiting and training new hires was about 15 months as a result of continual turnover.

Duke's management and training staff realized the current training program needed to be updated and made more flexible. Since ongoing system and technology upgrades necessitated constant changes in the material, ease of updating the content became an important factor in the redesign. Another factor was the desire to deliver the initial program as well as recurrent training, readily and consistently across all shifts. Another priority was to reduce expenses associated with training new hires by shortening actual time spent by trainees and instructors in the classroom as well as the time it takes for an employee to reach average proficiency.

Organizational Profile

Founded in 1904, Duke Power is one of the nation's largest investor-owned electric utility companies. The company has three nuclear generating stations and operates eight coal-fired stations, 31 hydroelectric stations, and numerous combustion turbine units. The leadership position Duke occupies in its industry is evident by its having won the prestigious Edison Award from the Edison Electric Institute an unprecedented three times. The company also consistently achieves top ranking among utility companies on the American Customer Satisfaction Index as published by the University of Michigan Business School and its partner associations.

Duke's excellence in safe and reliable operations is well-known and broadly recognized. The company is committed to improving the quality of life in the communities in which it operates through partnerships designed to enhance land and water resources surrounding power generation sites. As a responsible corporate citizen, Duke supports local improvement efforts, particularly in public education and the arts and sciences. One example of the company's educational thrust is the Energy Explorium at Duke's McGuire Nuclear Station near Charlotte. The Explorium offers schoolchildren, teachers, and the general public a hands-on opportunity to learn how electricity is generated and how to use energy wisely.

The Call Center

The customer call function at Duke Power originally began in a decentralized format with employees working in business offices throughout North and South Carolina. Each of these local offices housed eight to 10 employees who performed various functions from handling customer calls to line maintenance and repair. About 10 years ago, in an effort to reduce costs and streamline functions, Duke began closing most of its business offices and migrated all customer call functions to a centralized call center in Charlotte.

The company-owned call center, located in the university area north of Charlotte, was completed in 1991. Prior to building the center, Duke completed a business mapping process and had the center designed and built around these processes by a local contractor. The center is situated in a private setting within an upscale industrial park. The building uses as much natural light in the interior as possible, and all workstations and sound-masking systems are ergonomically designed. Although Duke is an electric utility provider, it does have sustainable power systems for use during outages. Table 1 gives the call center's performance statistics. Customers are informed about Duke Power's 24-hour, seven-day-a-week service through a variety of means, including bill inserts, the company's Website (www.DukePower.com), and telephone directories.

Customer calls are segmented and handled according to the following three types of calls:
- *basic calls:* requests for establishing electrical service for residential customers as well as billing questions, water levels at the lake, load control, or time use rates
- *intermediate:* calls from residential contractors and builders
- *complex:* calls from commercial accounts.

Technology

When customers dial any of Duke's customer service phone numbers, they are prompted by an electronic operator, or interactive voice response (IVR), to make selections concerning the nature of the call. The programmed selections distinguish between residential and commercial accounts and ask callers to key in their account numbers by punching on their telephone keypad. Calls are automatically forwarded in a tiered format to the correct call specialist. First-tier employees, or base call specialists, receive calls from residential customers, and the more difficult calls (from residential contractors and commercial accounts) are escalated to the second- and third-tier employees, respectively. Occasionally, customers make incorrect keypad selections, and the call is misdirected; it is then transferred internally to the appropriate call specialist.

The phone system technology allows the Duke employee receiving the call to view customer information on the computer screen just

Table 1. Call center performance statistics.

Schedule	24/7
Shifts	3 (inbound calls only)
Phone Representatives	550+
Management	One general manager; 27 coaches who supervise about 35 employees per shift. The coaches are assisted by team leads, who work as liaisons between the phone representatives and supervisory management, in a 15:1 ratio.
Call Volume	Approximately 8.5 million calls a year, or over 20,000 a day. Call volumes are cyclical and tend to be higher during electrical or snowstorms. During the winter of January 1998, the company answered five million calls in a two-week period. It is during such times that the remote business offices support the main center in handling overflow calls.
Average Call Handling Time	503 seconds

as the call is connected. The call specialist has immediate information concerning the caller's name and address, type of current service, billing information, and credit rating with Duke. Personal identification numbers are not needed since the call specialist can ask the caller specific questions about the account to verify identity. Internal transfers are kept to a minimum due to the phone system and Duke's desire that customer requests be handled by the first person receiving the call. Caller satisfaction is measured through transactional surveys conducted by an outside firm on a regular basis.

The center uses other forms of technology, such as fax and email, to communicate with customers. Specific employees are designated to handle these forms of communication. The company began offering a self-service option via its Website in mid-2000.

Recruiting Process

Duke Power originally began as a family business, and in many respects the company has maintained this atmosphere in its recruiting, hiring, and employment practices. The company's longstanding emphasis on customer service is an important element considered during the hiring process.

The company sources employees via the Web, newspapers, and referrals so that it constantly builds the pool of prospects for regular hiring as well as to increase staff during peak times. Employees are recruited for a specific shift and are trained during that shift, if possible. Most employees are needed to work full-time, although the company hires some part-time employees, many of them college students, to add flexibility to the shifts or to extend the range of the schedule. Duke, a nonunionized company, only uses internal recruiters to hire call center personnel.

Interviews

Duke uses a specific interview process, including preemployment screening, testing, and interviewing, prior to hiring. Duke first screens applicants via an automated phone interview based on a customized recruiting tool. If the applicant successfully completes this step, a recruiter invites him or her to the call center for a face-to-face interview with a human resource representative. At this time, HR gives the applicant a preemployment assessment. This online assessment indicates how well the individual will handle certain situations in the future. The interview also includes meeting with a coach to learn more about the job. Candidates selected for the position must undergo mandatory preemployment drug screening and a background verification of prior employment and education. The company requires a high school diploma or GED.

Job Description

The job description for the base call specialist requires certain skill sets the company considers vital to accomplishing organizational goals, such as excellent listening skills, using appropriate questioning techniques to determine customer needs, using computers and telephones simultaneously, basic math skills, and excellent communication skills. Perhaps customer service is the most important quality that Duke looks for and rewards. Historically, the company has provided exceptional service to customers and shareholders alike—a policy that has essentially forged the company's positive reputation.

Duke began a career pathing program for the base call specialists in 1999. The career path involves a potential progression from base call specialist to residential construction call specialist to the highest phone position of business and industry call specialist. Successful business and industry call specialists can be promoted to team lead and then coach.

Since employees can be promoted through several tiers of call handling, as well as into supervisory roles, the company uses various pay scales. Duke bases its starting pay for the base call specialists on the 50th percentile of the Southeastern U.S. pay range for those in similar positions. Additionally, the employee can earn 25 percent more pay in variable incentives, thus bringing the base pay to 75 percent of the current market rate.

Although the career pathing program is relatively new, it has had a positive impact on call specialist retention. The turnover rate for the base call specialist group is about 42 percent; however, this number includes internal moves and promotions. Only 22 percent of the base call specialists left the company altogether last year.

Training Program

Recognized as a regional corporate leader, Duke provides the training necessary for its employees to provide outstanding just-in-time service to its customers and shareholders. This level of service requires ongoing system upgrades, which, coupled with changes and improvements in business processes, has led to constant updates to the call center's classroom-style curriculum. As a result, the company has been under continual pressure both to train new hires and to retrain existing employees. Last year, call center management became concerned about the impact of increasing turnover and the constant struggle to train all employees as efficiently and effectively as possible. Therefore, in mid-1999, management decided to redesign the call center's training program to better meet the organization's short- and long-term needs.

Joni Truss, a 15-year Duke employee, was transferred to the call center in July 1999, to manage the training redesign. At the time, the training staff included six instructors and one instructional designer. Truss decided to redesign the basic curriculum first and then modify the training for the more advanced functions later. She wanted the curriculum to be based on skill sets employees actually use on the job and wanted to structure the content so that it could be learned as systematically as possible. In order to combat the difficulty of having to delay training until a class of 20 people was formed, Truss planned for the new curriculum to be self-paced and to allow for individual entry and exits. Having such flexibility would allow new employees to begin training almost immediately after their hire dates, and it would reduce time spent in the classroom by both trainees and Truss's staff. This method, Truss projected, would eliminate many of the difficulties inherent in training across shifts, such as inconsistencies in delivery and content as well as staff availability issues. According to Truss, one of the major challenges in the project was to run the existing program while the redesign was under way, a feat much like "changing a tire on a moving vehicle."

To achieve her stated goals, Truss reexamined an accomplishment-based curriculum the company had purchased previously and had used somewhat in the original training design. Although Duke considered using a large consulting firm to manage the redesign, Truss convinced senior management to hire the company representing the product she had previously used since she had worked with the vendor before and knew it was well respected in the human performance technology arena. Truss asked that the vendor supply the redesign process and part of the labor; the other part of the labor would come from her own staff. She wanted the members of her staff to work alongside the vendor so they could gain skills that would allow for future redesigns to be handled in-house at a substantial cost savings. About 60 percent of the base call specialist training was targeted for the redesign, and, of this amount, Truss's staff handled approximately 40 percent of the development.

The first step in the redesign involved a baseline analysis. Since the call process is basically a series of stimulus-response patterns, each phone call, including the information appearing on the computer screen, can be seen as stimuli that create a need for a response from the call specialist. Truss and her staff, along with the vendor, mapped out all call processes and sought to uncover all possible stimulus-response chains. In one instance, they discovered over 500 nonlinear operants for one particular process. This finding confirmed the complexity of the material needing to be learned and the magnitude of the project. Also during this phase, many covert behaviors, such as how effectively and efficiently employees complete input fields on the computer screen, were uncovered. A process using paradigms was used to transform the covert behavior into usable information for the training design.

Although most of the company's processes had been mapped previously by individual process owners, Truss discovered that most, if not all, of these processes converged at the phone specialist's desktop. Areas such as billing, collections, and electrical distribution are separate functions in the company; however, as the phone representatives work through customer issues, they are often caught in multiple or overlapping processes. Discrepancies about how the process should work created conflict among the departments involved. Since all of the company's processes are accounted for in the training, when these inconsistencies came to light during the redesign, the affected departments met informally to discuss and modify best practices. Refining the processes while the training was being redesigned resulted in more streamlined operations and a better training program.

After analyzing the company processes the base call specialists needed to support, Truss, her staff, and the vendor began the training design. The analysis phase had revealed the vastness of the information that the call specialists needed to access, and the training staff quickly realized that the trainees could not hold this universe of information reliably in memory. Therefore, Truss began to look for ways to provide electronic support, not only for the training environment, but also on the job. She provided Duke's internal information technology (IT) staff with general parameters about the type of product she needed to support the call specialists. After investigation, an IT staff member recommended a software package compatible with Duke's system that utilizes a built-in online help program. The company purchased the software, and it soon became central to the training redesign.

Truss's staff and the vendor scripted the knowledge base of the base call specialists, based on the documented best method for handling each company process, into the software by using varying levels of real-world simulations. The script is available, through a window on the computer screen, during every call. Other reference tools, such as online user manuals that provide background on certain topics, are also available. The phone specialists always have access to the online user assistance tool click by click, and, eventually, it will link to other reference tools. The tool provided the means for the training, including systems training, to be almost entirely self-paced, thus accomplishing several of Truss's primary objectives for the redesign.

After the design phase was completed, the development phase began with the creation of courses, modules, and units. During this phase, the vendor was available on an as-needed basis with Duke's training staff handling the bulk of the development. The final curriculum was completed in May 2000 and consists of four weeks of self-paced instruction with a few courses still being instructor led. One of the instructor-led courses concerns billing, and Truss decided to keep the course in this format since the technology supporting this process was slated to change. Eventually, all courses will be self-paced. During the self-paced portion of the training, a class manager is available to assist new employees on a one-to-10 ratio. The four-week training program includes a weeklong "nesting" period in which employees are given the opportunity to handle live phone calls under close supervision. The ratio between the facilitator and trainees begins at one to five and progresses to one to 15 before employees are released to work live calls by themselves. For evaluation purposes, five calls are monitored for quality per month.

In addition to technical training, the curriculum provides courses in other areas pertinent to the base call specialist position, such as providing customer service and handling irate customers. For the latter, call specialists are taught to redirect the caller's anger, and they can obtain assistance from a supervisor if necessary. However, actual wording of what to say to the customer has been imbedded in scripts, so no role-playing is used in the training. According to Truss, one of the most difficult topics to teach involves how to help the call specialists explain a higher-than-expected utility bill to a customer. This process can involve troubleshooting, using conflict resolution tools, and even requesting a company representative to go to the customer's house and to reread the electric meter in order to resolve the concern. Truss and her staff are always looking for new ways to improve telephone techniques. The content for some of these additional courses is delivered via off-the-shelf videos followed by classroom-based discussion for application, the intranet, and computer-based training, and one course is taught via CD-ROM. Additionally, the curriculum is evaluated after every group completes the training, and changes are made as necessary.

Duke also has processes in place to support new employees after they complete their training. The employees continue to use the same scripting on the job that was used in the training, a factor that ensures consistency among the specialists and provides for optimal quality in process handling. The Quality Assurance Team monitors at least five calls per month for each base call specialist. A major part of the monitoring involves whether or not the call specialists are actually using the script to best leverage each call. The quality assessor can parallel the call specialist by following the same script and noting what is being done correctly as well as any discrepancies. Any errors detected in the monitoring process lead to immediate feedback and potential retraining via the online user assistance tool. Since everything the specialist needs to know is in the online assistance tool, Duke does not offer any refresher courses; the information is continually at the employee's fingertips.

Duke motivates call specialists through a structured pay system and performance incentives and awards. The performance management metrics include a rating system leading to an annual performance review for each employee. Call specialists know what factors they will be measured against before they complete training since the performance criteria is based on the call monitoring sheets used in the training and while on the job. About a year ago, Duke changed the pay scale to a step-pay progression, with the call specialists receiving a pay increase every four months until they reach the midpoint of the salary range, usually at about one year of service. They also can earn up to 25 percent of their pay in variable compensation based on incentives.

Duke offers an employee incentive plan with cash payouts, usually a percentage of the employee's annual base pay, for achieving annual, corporate goals. The company's operational goals are broken down according to what the call specialists can do to achieve them. Buy-in for accomplishing overall call center goals is created through incentives, usually a monetary reward. The company plans for a distribution based on a specific percentage; however, more money can be given if certain criteria are met. Knowing that a year is a long time to wait, management usually establishes monthly incentive goals to help employees focus on short-term goals that support the overall annual goals. During these times, the company will make smaller payouts four to six times a year.

Short-term incentives and other performance awards are also used to motivate employees and reward them for going beyond expectations and providing exceptional customer service. These awards can include cash when a certain score is achieved on call monitoring, and everyone is eligible for the incentive. Due to scheduling for phone shifts, the company cannot offer days off, so Duke uses casual days as a similar type of reward. The company has a business-casual dress code, but employees are not allowed to wear jeans to work except as a performance reward for meeting individual or team goals. Duke also enthusiastically celebrates the annual National Customer Service week. The company selects a theme for the week and plans mini-celebrations daily. Supervisors leave small surprises, such as specialty chocolates, on every call specialist's desk. Other events have included a breakfast cart, group lunches, barbecue picnics, and food days.

Evaluation Process

Duke ultimately evaluates the training design based on how well the call center employees execute the agreed-upon service levels for other departments within the company and provide customer service. A balanced scorecard approach is used and is based on business goals and service level agreements. The goals of the call center are communicated via meetings, the intranet, and copies of the operational plan are distributed to all employees. The essential pieces for success include financial performance, operational excellence, customer service and satisfaction, and employee involvement in the transition to a competitive, deregulated environment. For example, to establish electric utility service, a call center representative takes the customer's request and performs the necessary computer work according to the predetermined process. Then, the request is handed off to field personnel so the process can be completed. Since the call specialist must capture the need properly, for evaluation purposes, approximately 70 percent weight is given to technical skills and 30 percent to customer service ability.

The methods and criteria for corrective action, when a call specialist is underperforming, include a performance improvement plan with a specified time to show progress. The coach determines the length of time needed for improvement on an individual case-by-case basis. Weekly coaching can lead to progressive corrective actions, sometimes culminating in termination.

Duke also offers a resource library, called the Learning Lab, for ongoing development. The lab contains books, videos, and CBT programs on various topics for additional development. Employees may use the lab on their own time, such as during lunch; however, there is no requirement for employees to use these resources. Coaches and team leaders reinforce learning, and employees can take sections of the training over repeatedly if necessary, or use other available resources.

Costs

Costs associated with the program can be understood via actual costs and realized savings. After the training design was completed, Truss was able to project the estimated cost of developing the program. She created the projections in the fall of 1999, and, at the time, the estimates included all foreseeable factors impinging on the redesign. Truss proposed a budget just under $500,000 to cover the expenses associated with the training redesign. The amount included all internal and contract labor, software, and other materials. It also included time spent by the vendor in developing the Duke training staff to become proficient instructional developers. Additionally, Truss projected that when revisions or additions were needed for the base call specialist training, the costs would be far less than for the initial project since she would be able to use her own staff as a pure labor expense.

In projecting the return-on-investment (ROI) for the completed program, Truss estimated a 1.18 percent ROI in the first year. These cost savings are shown in table 2.

Table 2. Cost savings calculations for training redesign.

Factor	Cost Savings
Reduce training time by one week. The calculation was based on the entry-level salary, loaded for benefits, for 200 new employees a year (conservative estimate).	$118,000
Reduce time needed for new employees to reach proficiency from 12 weeks to 8 weeks (with all courses self-paced).	$209, 000
Reduce average call handling time by 10 seconds per year per call specialist.	$249,000
Savings as a result of improved quality and customer satisfaction, and increased value of training staff.	Not quantified
Total	**$576,000**

Data Analysis

Since Duke maintained historical data on the original training program, it was possible to compare efficacies between the program designs. Truss had four major goals she wanted to achieve through the redesign:

- to reduce the time needed to train new hires by one week due to the self-paced delivery method
- to reduce the time needed for new employees to become proficient (average productivity) from 12 weeks to 8 weeks
- to reduce the average call handling time by 10 seconds per call specialist per year
- to realize cost savings from an improved quality and customer satisfaction perspective as well as the increased value of her staff to the company.

Truss's first goal was to reduce training time by one week. The former, classroom-based curriculum was designed for a five-week period. Truss was only too aware of the limitations of this program: Enough employees had to be hired at the same time in order to create a class, and the classroom delivery method, across all shifts, put a major strain on the availability and flexibility of the training staff. Therefore, with the introduction of the self-paced training program, Truss was able to reduce the time needed to deliver the content from five weeks to four weeks.

Truss's second goal was to reduce the time it takes for a new employee to become proficient, or to reach an average level of productivity, from 12 weeks down to eight weeks. Truss believed that the streamlined training would have a positive impact on the productivity and proficiency of the new hires, and the reduction in time would be achieved due to the self-paced nature of the training. The time to reach proficiency has been reduced from 12 weeks to seven weeks.

Third, Truss planned for the redesigned program to reduce average call handle time by 10 seconds per year per call specialist. However, due to a system change, the baseline for achieving this goal changed from the time Truss made the projections until the time the redesigned training was introduced. Unfortunately, the system change eliminates the possibility of quantifying any decrease in call handling time.

Truss's final goal was to realize savings by improving quality and customer satisfaction results. Additionally, Truss wanted to increase her staff member's skill levels so they could handle the redesign of the training for the other two call specialists groups. At the time of publication, the call quality scores had improved approximately three points in just six months after the redesign. Initially, Truss's staff was not trained in instructional design techniques, but after working closely with the vendor, her staff members were able to complete the development and are currently responsible for maintaining the program.

Results

The first group of new employees completed the redesigned curriculum in early June 2000. Due to scheduling conflicts, the redesigned program was inaugurated in less than optimal circumstances as it was introduced during a weekend shift. However, Truss needed the program to be flexible, so putting it afloat would only point out the seaworthiness of the new curriculum. In the first class of 23 new hires, two people struggled with the self-paced delivery method; and in the second class, only one of the 20 new hires elected to self-terminate employment at Duke. From May 1 through August 15, Duke held a total of seven classes, with 120 new hires completing the redesigned curriculum. Of these seven classes, six classes finished in four weeks and one class needed an additional week due to a major storm that interrupted the training schedule. One unexpected issue surfaced after the training: The trainees have higher quality immediately after training than they do after being on the phone for several months. This could be due to the recent effect of the training, or new employees may be taking shortcuts once they get on the job.

Truss has interviewed new employees to learn their opinions of the self-paced training delivery method and suggestions for it. On the basis of these conversations, in a typical class of 15 to 20 new hires, about five or six really enjoy the training, one or two struggle with the self-paced curriculum, and the remainder say they prefer a classroom style course, but are willing to complete the self-paced program. Almost all of the employees who have self-terminated have done so early in the training process. Truss realizes that the program does not accommodate all learning styles; however, she is confident that the training mirrors the real world since employees are expected to be self-directed and learn on their own and contribute to their own development.

Conclusions, Learnings, Recommendations

As a 10-year veteran in the call center arena, Duke Power's management saw very clearly how increasing competition for qualified employees and an inefficient training program would not adequately support the company in achieving a positive future state. With top management's support, Joni Truss, manager of human performance at the Customer Service Center, was able to create an out-of-the-box training curriculum for the entry-level base call specialists. The combination of supportive management and a training manager willing to plunge into a challenge resulted in a winning combination for Duke Power.

A serendipitous result of the redesigned curriculum is the importance of self-directedness in those successfully completing the training. Unfortunately, not enough data is available to determine the long-term success of this method; however, the company is investigating ways it can alter its recruiting strategy in order to source for self-directed behavior.

Each time the class is offered, Duke requests feedback from the new employees and the coaches and then feeds this data back into the program to continuously improve and streamline it. Truss has noted that initially some new employees tried to skim the self-paced material and really did not understand it or know what to do when quizzed. Therefore, after each course, stringent reviews are now conducted to ensure that employees have reviewed the material and that they are actually using it.

Although the redesign was originally based on estimates made well in advance of the actual beginning of the training, Truss is pleased with the time and expense savings. A lesson learned came in the form of making projections too far in advance, such as estimating the time needed to develop portions of the program prior to uncovering all variables. It was not until the vendor, and the Duke staff, analyzed extremely detailed tasks did they realize just how complicated some processes were and how long it would take to develop the training around them. In the future, Truss will continue to analyze the accomplishments the company wants the employees to achieve, list the job tasks based on the accomplishments, and then enter the details of the most complex task on a flow chart before estimating the time required to complete the training development. Truss is confident that her staff can develop the training on its own now, a major factor in any future cost savings.

Truss recommends that anyone desiring to make the transition to a self-paced training environment be aware that this environment is not for everyone. Additionally, portions of the training redesign at Duke Power have not resulted in the desired outcomes, but the company is continuing to work toward achieving its stated goals. With quality, customer service, cost containment, and employee retention at stake, call center management and training staffs must explore all avenues leading to continuous improvement.

Questions for Discussion

1. What are some of the challenges inherent in all call center training? To what extent did Duke Power overcome these challenges? What challenges would corporate training managers in larger companies or in different industries face that Truss did not?
2. Do you think other multimedia-based training has the same advantages or disadvantages as Duke Power's self-paced program with the online user assistance tool? Why or why not?
3. To what extent does self-directed learning have an impact on job performance?
4. What suggestions do you have for Duke Power on ways to incorporate what has been learned in the training redesign with the company's recruiting practices?

The Author

Trina A. Stephens is president of Human Resource Dynamics, located in Boiling Springs, North Carolina. The primary focus of her company is to assist small to midsized businesses with maximizing human resource development processes in order to achieve organizational objectives. Stephens is co-author of *Putting Corporate CLEP to Work for You and Your Employees,* published by the College Board, as well as numerous articles for business publications. She is the past president of the Valley's of Virginia Chapter of the ASTD. She received her M.A. in career counseling and her Ph.D. in adult and continuing education and human resource development from Virginia Polytechnic Institute and State University. She can be reached at Human Resource Dynamics, Inc., 3629 Franklin Road, Suite 203, Roanoke, VA 24014; phone: 540.345.9191; email: hrdynamicsinc@aol.com.

Benchmarking Call Centers

Financial Institution

Jon Anton

In the past five years, the call center has moved from a back-office cost center to the front line of the current corporate customer relationship management (also know as CRM) strategy. In this migration to CRM, the importance of the telephone service representative (often referred to as a TSR) has gone from the need for individuals with minimum skills at minimum pay to the need for the sophisticated knowledge worker of the present and future.

This case study describes a situation in which benchmarking was able to determine important gaps in call center performance and then pinpoint areas of improvement in human resource management. The case study focuses on a bank call center handling predominately inbound customer service calls.

Background

Technology has opened several new channels of communication between customers and companies. The two most popular with customers are email and the corporate Website. Management of customer relationships through these additional channels has added an *e* to CRM, namely electronic customer relationship management (now called e-CRM). With the additional management challenge of these new channels, the call center itself is in a transitory state as it moves more and more to becoming the e-business center of the future.

The importance of performance benchmarking has become mission critical now that top executives in both the public sector, or

This case was prepared to serve as a basis for discussion rather than to illustrate either effective or ineffective administrative or management practices. Names of places, organizations, or people have been disguised at the request of the author or organization.

government, and the private sector, or industry, are convinced that the e-business center is a strategic weapon for getting customers, keeping customers, and growing profitable customers.

Performance benchmarking is a structured, analytical method of comparing the performance of two or more call centers in order to determine best practice goals and to ensure competitive customer relationship management functionality leading to market dominance.

Performance benchmarking of a mission-critical company process, such as accounting, manufacturing, and shipping, has been around for years. The process is well documented and is a popular way to answer the question, "How good is good enough?" when it comes to the performance of a department or process within an organization. Benchmarking is always a structure gap analysis of performance metrics for organizations with similar characteristics. That is, it is logical to compare banks with banks, insurance companies with insurance companies, and the like.

By contrast, call center benchmarking is relatively new and was first initiated at Purdue University by the author in 1995 with a grant from IBM. After six years of research, the Purdue database of almost one terabyte of performance metrics is constantly being enhanced by new participants, and is now outsourced for data management, maintenance, and information distribution to a company called BenchmarkPortal (accessible at the Website BenchmarkPortal.com).

Call centers that wish to participate in benchmarking their performance can log onto the Purdue Website and enter their data, and then receive a complete set of benchmark reports similar to the examples discussed in this case study.

Why and How to Benchmark a Call Center

The primary reasons to benchmark a call center are as follows:

- Comparisons help to reduce the typical barriers to change. For instance, if you know your are 50 pounds overweight in comparison with your human peer group (that is, people with the same age, gender, and ethnicity), it is more likely that you will take some action to lose weight.
- You further enlarge performance gaps by calculating the dollar value of poor performance. For instance, it is much less likely that you will get management's attention if you publish a performance gap in an average talk time of 1.5 minutes per call than if you show that a performance gap of 1.5 minutes for each call compared with those of your peer group adds up to over a million dollar of excess cost each year.

- The main purpose of benchmarking is to help you select the one initiative that commits a minimum of company resources to achieve the best performance goals and objectives. Said in the modern vernacular, benchmarking helps you select the "low-hanging fruit."

Organizational Profile

This case study describes the benchmarking experience of a call center in a banking and financial services organization. This company, with $3 billion in assets, operated 22 call centers and employed 325 telephone service representatives who annually handled 4,524,000 calls. The primary functions of these representatives were customer service and handling complaints. Ninety percent of the calls they handled were inbound. The other 10 percent were follow-up outbound calls.

This North America bank participated in the Purdue benchmark research and has given its permission for the authors to use the data without revealing its identity. The Purdue benchmarking team selected a peer group, that is, a group of call centers that has a similar profile to this bank's call center. The profile delimiters used were industry segment (that is, banking and financial services), number of inbound calls handled (in this case, two million to five million calls), number of telephone service representatives (200 to 400), type of calls handled, and many more.

The next sections of this case study will
- give examples of the reports the bank's benchmark team used
- interpret the results
- explain the initiatives selected by the benchmarking team
- report on the final actual improvements in performance that resulted six months later.

The Peer Group Performance Matrix

The first report shows the peer group performance matrix shown in figure 1.

This report uses an efficiency index. An efficiency index is a combination of 10 performance metrics that are related to productivity. Examples would be average talk time, average after call work time, and calls per telephone service representative per shift.

To create this matrix, the efficiency index is plotted on the x-axis, and the effectiveness index is plotted on the y-axis. Call centers that are very inefficient at doing a very ineffective job for their companies are considered a corporate liability, whereas call centers that are very efficient and doing a very effective job for their companies are considered a corporate asset.

Figure 1. Peer group performance matrix, using an efficiency index.

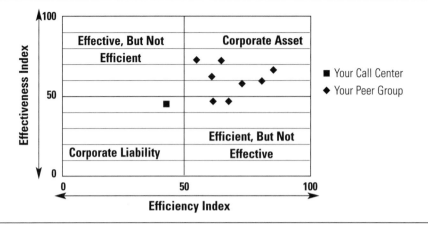

The performance matrix shows that the case study bank's call center is performing at the level of a corporate liability while six of its peer group call centers are able to achieve the status of a corporate asset. Two of the peer group call centers are in the efficient but not effective quadrant. It was immediately obvious to the call center benchmarking team that they must drill down (that is, look beneath the high-level numbers to the numbers used to calculate them) to determine what factors may be causing this less-than-acceptable performance.

Though the peer group performance matrix is not an actionable report, it is a high-level and accurate litmus test of the call center's ability to provide the customer-relationship-management best-practice standards of peer group call centers with the same business challenges. So, the next step was to find one or more of the possible root causes of the low performance.

The Inbound Performance Comparison Report

The first drill-down report is called the inbound performance comparison report. Figure 2 shows a partial listing from this report.

This report shows the following:

- call center performance metrics descriptions in the first column
- a column with the actual call center performance metrics of the case study bank (noted as "Your Center")
- the peer group medians and averages
- the best in peer group medians and averages
- the average for all participants.

Figure 2. Excerpt from the inbound performance comparison report.

Metric Description	Your Center Response	Peer Group Median	Peer Group Average	Peer Group Best Median	Peer Group Best Average	All Participants Median	All Participants Average
Average Speed of Answer (seconds)	35.0	20.0	32.2	12.5	17.1	25.0	33.3
Average Talk Time (minutes)	4.2	3.0	7.2	3.0	3.4	4.0	10.2
Average After Call Work Time (minutes)	3.0	1.0	5.3	1.0	1.1	2.0	6.8
Average Calls Abandoned (%)	7.0	3.0	5.0	2.0	2.8	4.7	5.5
Average Time in Queue (seconds)	54.0	35.0	44.3	16.0	18.4	34.0	43.2
Average First/Final Calls (%)	65.0	79.0	77.3	85.0	86.1	79.0	68.1
Average TSR Occupancy (%)	76.0	80.0	79.4	87.0	89.1	79.0	74.9
Average Adherence to Schedule (%)	81.0	89.0	87.8	92.0	95.3	84.1	86.0
Average Calls/Shift/TSR (calls)	58.0	70.0	83.2	85.0	86.5	70.0	69.2
Average Attendance (%)	75.0	90.0	88.7	95.0	87.7	88.3	86.9

The peer group best is the top 10 percent of a peer group.

For brevity purposes, this excerpt shows only 10 call center performance metrics. Those in this sample highlight HR management opportunities, the main topic of this case study. It immediately became clear to the benchmarking team that the case study call center is underperforming on the following HR-related metrics:

- average speed of answer
- average calls abandoned
- average time in queue
- average first/final calls
- average telephone service representative occupancy
- average adherence to schedule
- average calls per shift per telephone representative.

At this stage of the drill-down research by the benchmarking team, it was already becoming clear which metric may be having the biggest impact on performance. The most important caller satisfaction driver is the ability of a call center to answers callers' questions on the first call with no transfers and no callbacks. In figure 2, this metric is called the "average first/final calls" (also sometimes called "average once and done calls"). The case study bank's score is 65 percent, compared with the score of 77.3 percent for the peer groups of banks. The difference of 12.3 percent may appear small, but when the cost of this lack of performance is calculated for this bank, it totals over $2 million each year. That expense makes it worth launching an improvement initiative.

The Performance Ranking Report

The second drill-down report is called the peer group ranking report. Figure 3 gives a partial listing of this report.

This report gives the benchmarking team an even more detailed look at how the case study bank compares, metric for metric, with its peer group of banks. For instance, when it comes to blocked calls, the case study bank is actually doing rather well, performing in the 95.7 percentile and ranking second. However, in the important performance HR management metric of telephone representative occupancy, the case study bank is only ranked 11th, and only in the 18th percentile.

This report is focused on selecting the one metric that may be causing the most damage to performance—that is, finding the lowest hanging fruit—so management can direct a focused budget for an improvement initiative. Not shown in figure 3 is that the case study

Figure 3. Excerpt from the peer group ranking report.

Metrics ▶	Blocked Calls	Adherence	ASA	ATT	Abandoned	Queue Time	Occupancy
Your Percentile ▶	95.7%	26%	87%	22%	52.1%	74%	18%
Rank 1	.04%	95%	5	2.2	0%	10	91
2	**1.85%**	94%	7	3.6	2%	11	88
3	2.81%	92%	10	3.7	2%	13	86
4	3.05%	91%	**15**	4.2	2%	15	85
5	3.17%	90%	22	4.9	3%	16	82
6	4.84%	90%	25	5.1	4%	**20**	77
7	5.80%	89%	31	5.3	5%	32	73
8	5.82%	88%	31	6.6	**6%**	36	71
9	6.45%	86%	50	7.3	7%	39	68
10	7.78%	**82%**	60	8.5	7%	42	63
11	8.44%	77%	68	**9.1**	9%	45	**60**

bank ranks at the bottom, having had the absolute worst performance, on the metric of "average first/final calls." That initiative became the focus of the bank's benchmarking team.

From Performance Gaps to Solution Initiative

The final report is called the gap versus solution optimizer report. A partial listing of this report appears in figure 4.

This report gives the benchmark participant a listing of all gaps in excess of 20 percent (that is, the major ones) plus a list of potentially applicable solutions to reduce each gap. The figure lists only one such gap—"percent of once and done calls"—although there were a total of eight major gaps in performance at the bank's call center in the case study.

From the previous reports, the case study benchmarking team decided that the biggest negative gap in performance seems to be the average first/final calls, or "once and done calls." The gap versus solution optimizer report then becomes a management aid to select that one solution that may produce the best results with the minimum corporate resource.

This reports lists 11 solutions that could be implemented in the order of most desirable through least desirable on the basis of the optimal decision index. This index is calculated by statistically averaging the most important issues that managers should consider when selecting any improvement initiative, as follows:

- *Cost per seat:* Many solutions are priced on the bases of cost per seat. Knowing this factor allows the manager to quickly determine if there is enough money in the budget to even consider the initiative.
- *Implementation time:* This is an estimate of the average implementation time to complete the installation of the solution. Most managers prefer to select initiatives that can be implemented within approximately six months.
- *Risk factor:* Most managers are risk averse. The risk factor has been developed over time by discussing solutions with those who have already implemented a solution. Sometimes high-risk solutions are worth undertaking, but only in light of the other decision factors.
- *Gap impact factor:* This factor gives an indication of the percent of the gap that will be reduced by the successful implementation of a particular solution.
- *Return-on-investment (ROI):* This is the standard ROI equation that decision makers use most often in selecting one solution over another.

Figure 4. Excerpt from gap versus solution optimizer report.

Solution	Cost Per Seat ($)	Implement Time (days)	Risk Factor (0–100)	Gap Impact (%)	ROI (%)	Optimal Decision
Applicant Testing	100	30	40	20	374	6.49
Skill Based Routing	400	50	50	75	315	4.51
Applicant Screening	250	40	30	30	184	2.18
CT Integration	900	120	75	90	137	1.91
Value Based Routing	400	60	60	55	128	1.49
Monitoring/Coaching	300	60	40	65	118	1.33
Product Training	600	90	65	35	91	1.01
Expert Systems	1500	180	95	55	89	.94
Contact Tracking	3000	120	85	50	64	.85
Performance Comp	300	30	10	15	64	.65
CB Training	600	90	35	35	53	.61

From the gap versus solution optimizer report it becomes clear that applicant testing and skill-based routing are high on the list of potential improvement initiatives. In this particular example, the bank's benchmarking team received management's approval to pursue both initiatives. The team prepared specifications, issued requests for proposal (also called RFP), selected vendors, and launched and successfully completed the initiatives.

Results and Conclusions

Six months after the successful installation and implementation of the two improvement initiatives, the team tabulated the following results:
- The percent of first/final calls improved by 11.6 percent.
- The average time in queue was reduced by 2.8 percent.
- The average TSR occupancy was improved by just over 6 percent.
- Calls per TSRs per shift were increased by 9.4 percent.
- Caller satisfaction rose by almost 7 percent.

The bank in this case study spent approximately $600,000 for the two improvement initiatives, including the selection process, the cost of the software and hardware products, the training costs of the TSRs, and the installation services costs from a third-party integrator. When the improved metrics were converted to new revenue, reduced operating cost, and customer satisfaction, the estimated ROI was in excess of 100 percent in 16 months of operation.

In conclusion, benchmarking cannot guarantee the success of any improvement initiative. However, this case study does prove that by scientifically selecting initiatives based on hard facts, not just personal intuition, or gut feel, management can effectively target improvements that have the maximum impact on the company's bottom-line profits.

Questions for Discussion

1. What is performance benchmarking and why is its implementation critical to the success of call center management?
2. Discuss the importance of a peer group in performance benchmarking. What factors should be considered when selecting peer groups?
3. What is an efficiency index, and how does it help call center management deliver best practice standards in customer relationship management?
4. How does the gap versus solution optimizer report help call center management select performance improvement initiatives?
5. What are some ROI factors that should be considered when selecting one performance improvement solution over another?

The Author

Jon Anton is the director of benchmark research at Purdue University's Center for Customer-Driven Quality. He specializes in enhancing customer service strategy through inbound call centers and e-business centers, using the latest in telecommunications (voice) and computer (digital) technology. He has been the principal investigator of the annual Purdue University Call Center Benchmark Research Report. Anton has developed techniques for calculating the ROI for customer service initiatives and has assisted over 400 companies. Based on the analysis of this data, Anton is the author of "The Purdue Page" in *Call Center Magazine* each month, plus the "Dr. Jon Benchmarks" in *Call Center News* each month. In October 2000, Anton was named to the Call Center Hall of Fame. In January 2001, he was selected for the industry's Leaders and Legends Award by *Help Desk 2000*. He has published 75 papers and seven professional books on customer service and call center methods in industry journals. He can be reached at 1532 South Campus Courts-E, Purdue University, Lafayette, IN 47907; 805.934.1004, extension 18; email: drjonanton@benchmarkportal.com.

Suggested Readings

Anton, J., and David Gustin. (2000). *Call Center Benchmarking*. West Lafayette, IN: The Purdue University Press.

Davis, R.I., and J.W. Kincaide. (1994). *How to Prepare for and Conduct a Benchmark Project*. Washington, DC: Department of Defense, The Electronic College of Process Innovation.

www.BenchmarkPortal.com. Purdue University Benchmark Website.

The Psychological Impact of Change and Reengineering in a Call Center

The Braun Consumer Service Center

Jon Anton, Julie Kuliopulos, and Natalie L. Petouhoff

When a company's goal is to provide world-class customer service to its callers, training and managing reengineering initiatives are a critical part of the call center manager's job. The necessary changes that occur to remain competitive in a global market may have a substantial psychological impact on call center employees and may, in turn, also directly affect the service customer and customer retention.

The psychological impact of change on employees creates emotional ups and downs. Managing these emotional swings can make or break the success of the overall reengineering project. For example, when the human aspect of change is not considered part of the reengineering planning, there are impacts to the schedule, implementation costs, and lower return-on-investment for the new technology and processes. Often, employees do not use many of the features of the new technology, producing less-than-expected reengineering results. This case study focuses on the psychological impact of a reengineering initiative and offers practical suggestions for other call center managers to implement when preparing training around major improvements and changes to their call center.

Organizational Profile

Braun is a premier manufacturer of oral care products, shavers, coffeemakers, food preparation systems, and ThermoScan ear thermometers. The Braun Consumer Service call center handles over 200,000 inbound consumer calls annually, with call volume increasing at approximately

This case was prepared to serve as a basis for discussion rather than to illustrate either effective or ineffective administrative and management practices.

20 percent per year. Prior to reengineering, Braun had a basic in-house consumer contact system that offered no reporting or corporate support and that recorded only the consumer's name, address, and general text. Braun's management decided to invest in a major reengineering effort that would replace that system and would involve numerous changes to the existing call center processes.

The decision of what computer hardware and software system to use was simplified by Braun management's desire to use one that would be compatible with the system used by the Gillette Corporation, its parent company and alliance partner in the United States. Gillette had customized and implemented a comprehensive call center automation system two years earlier and had experienced notable success in call center effectiveness and productivity.

Introduction

People typically react to change, whether change at work or on a personal level, with some feelings of stress and discomfort and, if the change is managed well, with some happiness or elation as well. In creating ambitious goals or reengineering the way a company does something, managers should expect employees to move outside of their comfort zone when the process is put into place. This case study addresses the emotional reactions employees feel as they try to achieve a new level of performance. Managers should take these responses into account as they select, train, and hire new call center employees.

In selection, one needs to assess candidates for flexibility and openness to change. In the training process, call center managers need to include and communicate the human dynamic issues that occur when change happens. Also, because call centers are such an integral part of a company's business, companies must reward as part of the performance evaluation process those employees who embrace the changes call centers make to provide excellent customer service.

The Human Reaction to Change

Consider the following learning experiences:
• learning to drive a car
• learning to snow ski downhill
• learning to speak a foreign language
• learning to play a musical instrument
• learning to fly an airplane.

Many people have similar reactions as they learn these skills. They have a high level of enthusiasm and optimism when they begin, followed by stress and frustration during the difficult learning phase, followed finally by joy and exhilaration upon mastery of the new skill. We, the authors, have found that this same emotional upswing, followed by an emotional downswing, followed by an emotional upswing occurs in the process of reengineering a call center with new technology. We call this psychological phenomenon the *Valley of Tears*. Whether a company is undergoing a major technology change in a call center or a smaller improvement project, managers must understand that unanticipated and painful surprises are likely, and they must train employees in these issues.

In our research and real-time reengineering experiences, we have found the Valley occurs regardless of the technology application or process improvement being implemented at a call center. It is just as common for the Valley to occur if a company is implementing changes in telecommunications equipment, computer hardware, or computer software or even if the change is to the work flow or processes by which work gets done. The reason for this is because changes to technology or process change how people do what they do at work and that change in and of itself is disorienting. Forty percent of the working population is adverse to change.

By understanding and anticipating the Valley of Tears, managers and their team members can prepare mentally for the difficulties that may occur. A well-trained team can recognize the issues as they are coming up and can be proactive about solutions and options, pulling together and remaining productive. If the team perseveres through the Valley of Tears, it is likely that the implementation will be successful with a rewarding amount of completion euphoria.

Figure 1 shows how change can affect basic job functions, and figure 2 shows employees' typical reactions to the changes being suggested. This human dynamic and reaction to change can cause an implementation to go awry if insufficient attention is paid to it, as figure 3 shows. These risks can be managed if the human dynamic of change is considered as part of the implementation as a change management program.

Gaining the Data to Show the Value of a Change Management Plan

The Braun Consumer Service Center underwent a major expansion of call center capabilities and a substantial improvement in effectiveness by the integration of more complex and more robust call center computer hardware and software. To observe and record the existence of the Valley of Tears, the 14-member process improvement team at Braun, led by Julie Kuliopulos, kept a weekly diary of how it felt about its endeavor throughout the difficult and sometimes frustrating implementation phase. The team used a frustration scale that ranged

Figure 1. Change affects the way people do their jobs.

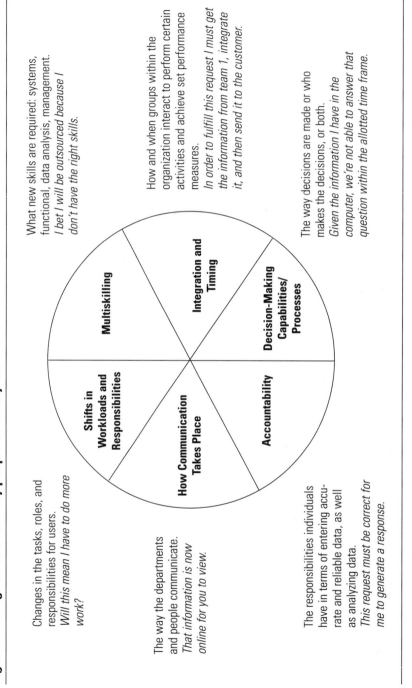

What new skills are required: systems, functional, data analysis, management. *I bet I will be outsourced because I don't have the right skills.*

How and when groups within the organization interact to perform certain activities and achieve set performance measures. *In order to fulfill this request I must get the information from team 1, integrate it, and then send it to the customer.*

The way decisions are made or who makes the decisions, or both. *Given the information I have in the computer, we're not able to answer that question within the allotted time frame.*

Multiskilling

Integration and Timing

Decision-Making Capabilities/ Processes

Shifts in Workloads and Responsibilities

How Communication Takes Place

Accountability

Changes in the tasks, roles, and responsibilities for users. *Will this mean I have to do more work?*

The way the departments and people communicate. *That information is now online for you to view.*

The responsibilities individuals have in terms of entering accurate and reliable data, as well as analyzing data. *This request must be correct for me to generate a response.*

Figure 2. People react to changing process and technology.

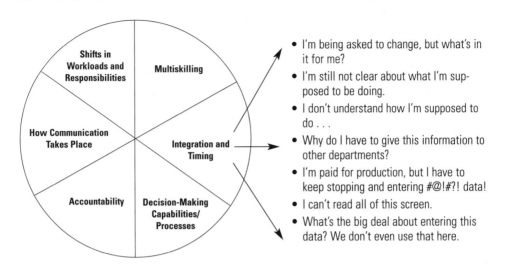

- I'm being asked to change, but what's in it for me?
- I'm still not clear about what I'm supposed to be doing.
- I don't understand how I'm supposed to do . . .
- Why do I have to give this information to other departments?
- I'm paid for production, but I have to keep stopping and entering #@!#?! data!
- I can't read all of this screen.
- What's the big deal about entering this data? We don't even use that here.

from one, a hostile feeling of frustration for the results at the end of the week, to 10, a very satisfied experience at the end of the week.

The purpose of recording the emotions through a reengineering project is to document the reality of the human reaction to change and its effect on the expected results. We felt that the documentation of this reaction to change would help call center managers and employees handle major technology or process improvements, or both, and also provide the evidence often needed to convince executives of the need for a change management plan as part of the reengineering budget and plan. In fact, Ed Oakley and Doug Krug (1991) reported that 85 percent of executives say they are disappointed by the efforts of reengineering projects, but do not know or understand that one of the major factors in failed reengineering projects is how well the human dynamic of change was handled. By reporting our data on the Braun reengineering project, we felt anyone involved in a change project would benefit and be even better prepared for the psychological challenges of reengineering because the same pattern of emotional response to change happens in every change project.

The Valley of Tears

The graph of the Valley of Tears in figure 4 illustrates that the team at Braun started out feeling good about getting the funding for the long-awaited reengineering initiative. The funds were approved

Figure 3. Human reactions create risks that need to be assessed and managed.

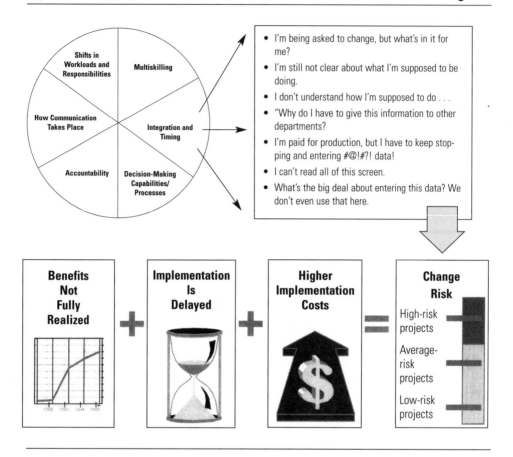

after weeks of compiling the required documentation, which included return-on-investment (ROI) calculations, a functional requirements description, call work flows, and product and system specifications. However, when the Braun team members detailed all the tasks that they needed to accomplish in a short period of time, they quickly became overwhelmed and emotionally frustrated. The comments from team members could be summed up in one statement, "How could we possibly do all the work that was necessary along with our normal day-to-day jobs and meet the high expectations that the team and the company had set?" The task at hand seemed impossible and no longer as interesting or invigorating. The goal of a more efficient call center with better customer service was lost in a sea of emotions and unrealizable expectations.

Figure 4. Valley of tears.

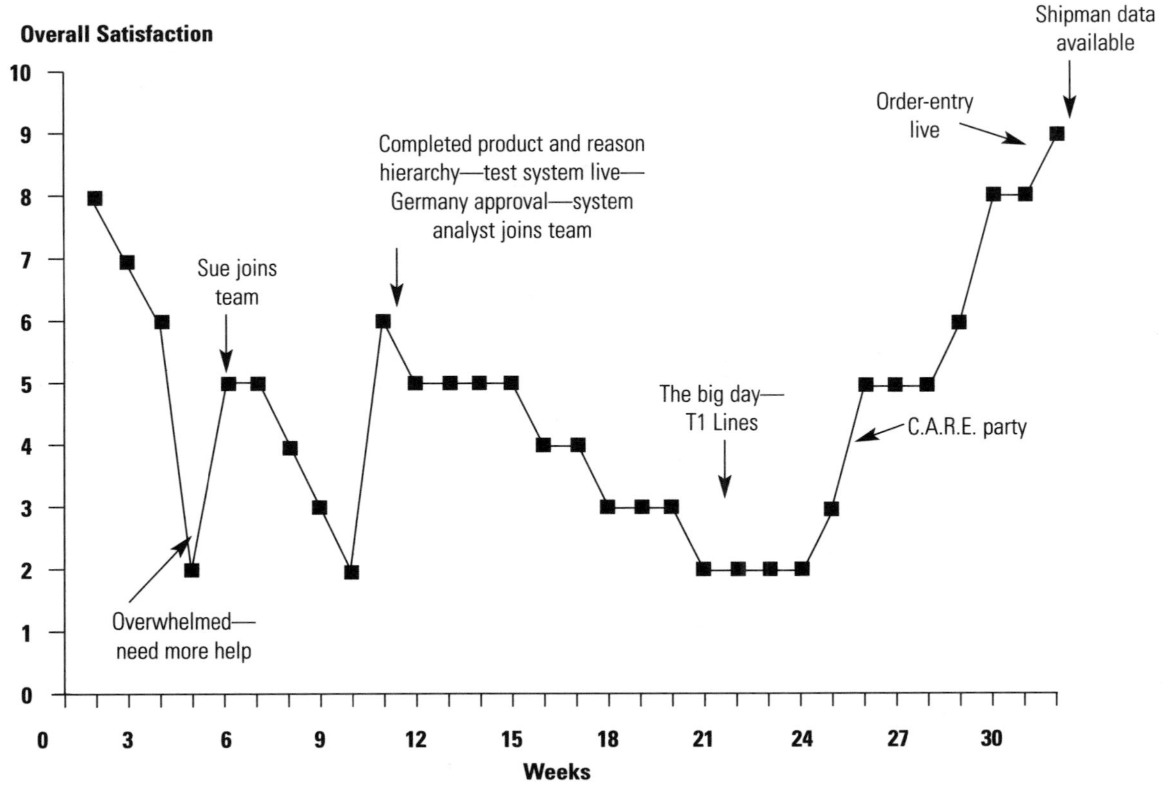

Overall Satisfaction
10
9
8
7
6
5
4
3
2
1
0
0
3
6
9
12
15
18
21
24
27
30
Weeks
Overwhelmed—
need more help
Sue joins
team
Completed product and reason
hierarchy—test system live—
Germany approval—system
analyst joins team
The big day—
T1 Lines
C.A.R.E. party
Order-entry
live
Shipman data
available

Solutions to the Human Reaction to Change

It is important for some members of a team to be naturally optimistic. Typically, about 80 percent of a team reacts negatively to change, with 20 percent or less feeling good about the change. To facilitate the optimism in the midst of the Valley of Tears, the team leadership added to the implementation team a key customer service representative (CSR), who was an eternal optimist. The value the optimist brought to the team was a wealth of knowledge and enthusiasm, which got us quickly back on track. We then proceeded back into the Valley of Tears. The team went all out, working late hours and weekends. The team was feeling the strain, but because it had been aware of the Valley of Tears, the members expected that the process of change was going to be tough. They understood that the feelings they were experiencing were temporary and normal for a team creating a change project.

A huge boost out of the Valley of Tears occurred each time we accomplished a key milestone. We had completed a large portion of the new system design and had a configured prototype system that was loaded on several CSR workstations. The feeling was great as we walked through the call center and saw CSRs properly testing the new system and enjoying the new features. It truly gave us the feeling that we were really going to make it happen! At the same time, we were able to hire a systems analyst, a newly created position. Having someone in that position for the first time reduced the pressure and relieved the frustration of making sure the system would perform.

We pushed on with weekly meetings of the process improvement team and our regularly scheduled weekly department meetings. In these meetings we made a point of communicating our progress, and we focused on the solutions to obstacles, or what we called our show stoppers. Open and honest communication kept us focused on activities that were critical to our success and that focus kept us on budget and deadline and within the scope of the project. We used the department meetings to keep everyone informed and working toward the same goal. Everyone knew what the goal was and why it was so important to accomplish it. An added advantage was that because everyone understood the Valley of Tears phenomenon, the team remained focused on the tasks to be completed. It would have been easy for frustration to overwhelm various team members, and that could have turned to blame or anger and gotten the team off track. The team's understanding of the inevitable emotional swings kept the members motivated to work together for the common goals.

By being in communication with the whole center about the changes, the employees proactively wanted to be involved in creating the new center. In fact the CSRs volunteered for product specialist positions, taking accountability for product categories in the new system and making sure that call work flows were completed for every possible reason a consumer might contact the call center. Each specific product category had to be represented in the new system and all assigned products were properly represented with informational scripts. Other CSRs volunteered to test the new system and to put it through its paces via beta-site testing. There was an incredible team spirit that you could feel just by walking through the call center. This would not have been possible if CSRs had not felt completely involved and in control of the changes that were happening to their job and ultimately to them.

Opening Day and the Need for Continued Change Management Awareness

When the big day came to use the new system, the team was ready! The members had a new system with well-trained CSRs who were excited and enthusiastic about using the new technology and following the new procedures they had helped to build. Our system documentation was complete, and the system vendor was there with us for the opening day. For additional insurance, we even invited extra Braun supervisors and managers (wearing their tennis shoes) on ready alert to assist with any possible problem as it occurred.

We had only one real problem: Customers' wait time was 20 minutes to 30 minutes, and the number of customers waiting kept building from 15 to 20 up to as many as 25. We expected a learning curve with the new system, but this backup was unthinkable. Everyone attributed it to the new system, but it turned out that two T1 phone lines had gone down the same day we began the new system. Because of this non-system failure, we lost 25 percent of our call handling capacity.

After the first full month of entering data into the system, we took all the data that went into the system that month and published our first report. With this major milestone under our belts, we celebrated the accomplishment with a party for the entire department. Everyone, including the vendor and senior management, went to an off-site restaurant for a gala event, with balloons filling the room and sweatshirts made up for everyone. We created a banner with pictures from the party and posted it on the department bulletin board to carry on the feeling of triumph. Celebrations during and throughout the implementation of the new system helped to sustain the enthusiasm and the employees' pride, which led to greater productivity.

We had high hopes for the entire system to go live at the same time, but the order entry system was not added until phase two of the system implementation and reengineering. When our order entry system went live, we really started to come out of the Valley. CSRs toggled back and forth between the new consumer contact system and the old order entry system for the first two months (not very elegant!), making sure that the new system could support the requests. While this can be a cumbersome process, running legacy systems along with the new system is common practice to ensure good customer service.

We completed our implementation and were out of the Valley of Tears when we finally had shipment data available in the new system. Shipment data gave us our analytical tool. The number of consumer comments for a product could now be compared to the total number of products that we shipped over the previous 12-month period, allowing for the factoring out of returns and heavy atypical shipping months, such as December. This analytical process is often called normalizing the caller data. Up until this point, we were reporting actual numbers, which were of interest, but were not actionable to improve customer service.

Where Theory and Reality Meet

This section focuses on the theory of team development stages, the typical behaviors from team members, the productivity of a team's work, and suggested behaviors for team leaders to help the team adjust through the various stages.

Figure 5 compares the various stages of team formation with those that occur when a person goes through a loss. The various stages of team development are as follows:
- forming
- storming
- norming
- performing
- transforming.

As a team forms and grows, team theory predicts there will be various stages of productivity and emotions because teams are made up of people who have predictable reactions to change. An understanding of these stages can keep a team from overreacting to normal group problems and from setting unrealistic expectations that can only lead to frustration. Team theory also states that it takes a team effort to reach the performing stage of team development and stay there.

It is most important to note that the actual data measured in the Braun Call Center Reengineering project by Julie Kuliopulos (figure 4)

Figure 5. Stages of team development and stages of human loss through time.

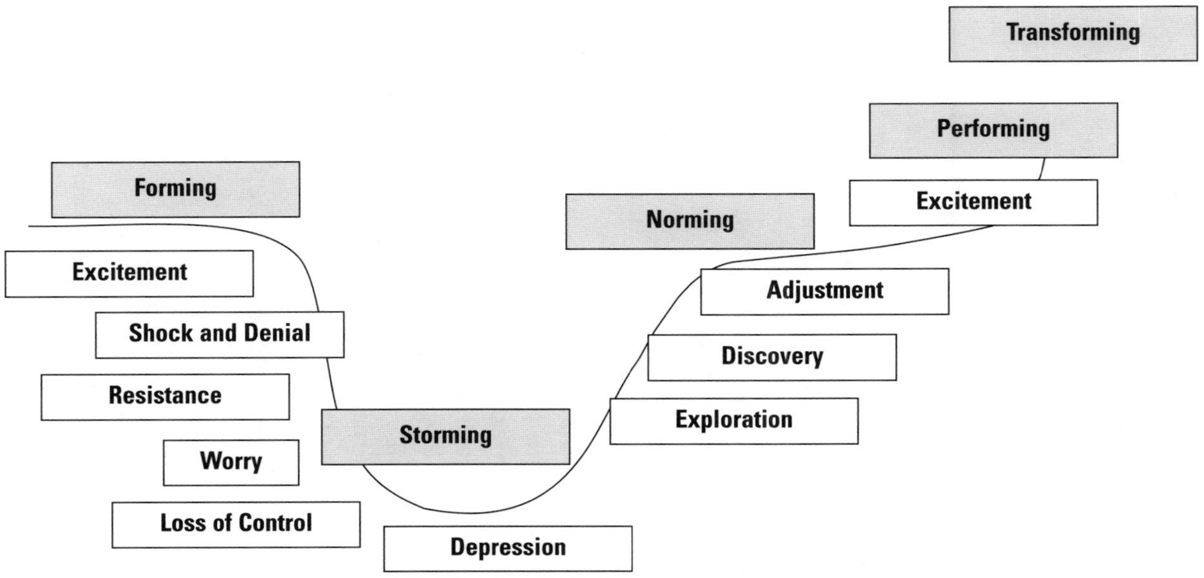

matches the stages of team development and productivity (figure 5). The graph in figure 5 closely depicts the data observed by Kuliopulos and the Braun team, showing that data matches the stages of team development, emotions, and productivity for any one Valley of Tears cycle. This match moves this discussion from the theoretical to the workplace, providing proof that the phenomenon of the Valley of Tears is real and may have a direct affect on a project's success if the team and its leader do not understand the effect of human dynamics on change.

Cycles Inside of Cycles

It is imperative to recognize that a team may move through all these development stages when facing a new issue. This means that there can be a cycle of the Valley of Tears within an overall Valley of Tears team development cycle. This cycle within the cycle can be created by a range of things in a long-term project. For example, a loss of a team member who is critical to the team, a delay in hardware or software delivery that throws off the schedule, or unpredicted issues that come up during implementation may create a minicycle within the larger Valley of Tears and team development cycle. It is typical to see dips in the emotional response of a team over the lifetime of a project.

Suggestions for Minimizing the Valley of Tears Effect

Table 1 provides a quick guide to the stage of team development. In each stage are listed the general types of team member emotions, the level of productivity or team work that can be expected in that stage, and suggested types of leadership actions that can help a team move forward through the stages to successfully complete the project. In this case study, the Braun team and leaders followed this type of program and completed a very successful reengineering project.

Change Management: People, Process, and Technology

New technologies accelerate the demands for change, including faster communications, more detailed and timely information about customers, and more precise measurements of cost and quality. Management must consider the triad of people, process, and technology in order to maximize the ROI for implementing state-of-the-art technology and process. Companies often buy the best technology available, only to find later that they do not need it or even the basic functionality of the system. A comprehensive change management program is required to guide change in the workplace.

A change management program looks at the whole change project. The following is a list of recommended actions for management

Table 1. Suggested leadership behaviors and productivity expectations.

Team Stages	Team Members' Emotions	Team Work or Productivity	Leadership Behavior Suggestions
Forming	• Generally eager • Anxious about why they are there, what's it in for them • Dependent on the leader	• Focusing on defining goals and tasks • Low task accomplishment	• Provide information • Develop skills of team • Clarify roles and goals
Storming	• Feelings of frustration • May have negative reactions to other team members and leader • Experience confusion • Morale dips	• Tasks disrupted by conflicts and discontent • Showing increasing task accomplishment and skill development	• Highly supportive behaviors • Listen to team members more • Support and resolve conflict resolution • Provide positive feedback
Norming	• Ways of working together become clearer • Feelings of mutual respect and trust evolve • Feel pleased with task completion	• Task accomplishment increases • Team members understand the task and output increases	• Decreased direction needed • Help team members to develop skills confidence • Encourage group to assume more responsibility • Communicate more
Performing	• Eager to be part of team • Feel confident about the goals • Work well together • Communicate openly and freely • Feel positive about team accomplishments	• High level of output • Task feels easier • Skill level is higher • Work more efficiently	• Continue to monitor goals and performance • Take a less active role in the team's regular operation; let them run things and be in control • Support members in taking a leadership role in problem solving
Terminating or Continuing	• Concern about project ending • Feel a sense of loss • Feel strong sense of accomplishment	• Output may decrease • May be increased output to meet final deadlines	• Provide support to team • Give positive feedback • Go through lessons learned • Communicate next steps

to consider as part of a change management program before, during, and after a major reengineering initiative at a call center:

- *Department team training:* Prepare awareness training about the human reaction to change; ask employees how they feel about change and how they feel they can contribute to the success of the change. Make the change project part of the performance evaluation process so that employees who embrace the change and help to move it forward are rewarded.
- *Department communication:* Prepare your staff for the changes that are taking place around them; communicate the vision and get buy-in to the project.
- *Team selection:* Have representation on your team from your internal information technology department, have supervision and representatives from the call center, and have your vendor with key stakeholders who have a vested interest in seeing the project succeed.
- *Team meetings:* Have regular team meetings to communicate and update team members. These may include the introduction of simple stress reduction techniques that could be done on the job, such as breath and stretching exercises, visualization, and positive self-talk. Professional athletes use many of these techniques.
- *Detailed task list:* List all required tasks in the beginning of the implementation and constantly update them, including the responsible team member, the target completion date, and percentage of progress to date.
- *Celebrate!* Celebrate your milestones to give your staff the feeling of accomplishment they deserve.

Recommendations for Realistic Reengineering Implementations

The following are planning issues the reader might consider when confronted with a major reengineering initiative:

- *Compromise:* It may not be possible to have everything available in a new system on day one. Schedule a phased implementation approach if possible.
- *Time during low volume:* If possible, time a switch to the new system during a low call volume period.
- *Convert history:* In order to do trend analysis, which an audience will want to see, convert at least 18 months of data from the old system.
- *Communication:* Keep the organization informed of what the goal is, why it is important, what can go wrong, and how things will change with the new system and the value those changes will bring to them. Constantly articulate a clear vision of what the call center will be

like when the final system is in place and how important those changes are to creating and keeping good customers.

- *Previous user experience:* Find a current user of the new technology and learn from that person.
- *Expect start-up bugs:* Try to work through bugs with a test system, but expect a few things to still need ironing out.
- *Involve reps in implementation:* Reps are the closest to the customers. They know what problems exist in the current system and what works. Ask them, involve them, and reward them.
- *Get buy-in from major audiences:* As early as possible, make sure the system in the works will meet the needs of the major audiences (stakeholders, executives, customers).
- *Understand the Valley of Tears:* Get everyone involved in minimizing it where possible!

Conclusions

At the conclusion of the project at Braun, Kuliopulos observed that, "As I look back I find it hard to remember all the bumps and bruises we experienced along the way. The first thing that comes to mind is the successful day when we switched over to the new system and the excitement that filled our call center. There is no doubt the implementation went easier because we understood, anticipated, and dealt with the Valley of Tears."

The reengineering initiative was a complete success and now delivers world-class customer service through a combination of wonderfully trained CSRs, well-developed processes, and excellent technology. Though the experience was tough and a lot of work, the noteworthy results are the reward for everyone involved.

Questions for Discussion

1. What is the impact of not considering people's feelings when going through a corporate change?
2. What is the fallout of people's poor attitude toward change?
3. How can a call center manager anticipate the issues around a reengineering project?
4. What are proactive steps a call center manager can take to make a reengineering program more acceptable to people and therefore more successful?
5. What are the proactive steps call center employees can take to embrace the changes in a reengineering of their call center?

The Authors

Jon Anton is the director of benchmark research at Purdue University's Center for Customer-Driven Quality. He specializes in enhancing customer service strategy through inbound call centers and e-business centers, using the latest in telecommunications (voice) and computer (digital) technology. He has been the principal investigator of the annual Purdue University Call Center Benchmark Research Report. Anton has developed techniques for calculating the ROI for customer service initiatives and has assisted over 400 companies. Based on the analysis of this data, Anton is the author of "The Purdue Page" in *Call Center Magazine* each month, plus the "Dr. Jon Benchmarks" in *Call Center News* each month. In October 2000, Anton was named to the Call Center Hall of Fame. In January 2001, he was selected for the industry's Leaders and Legends Award by *Help Desk 2000*. He has published 75 papers and seven professional books on customer service and call center methods in industry journals. He can be reached at 1532 South Campus Courts-E, Purdue University, Lafayette, IN 47907; 805.934.1004, extension 18; email: drjonanton@benchmarkportal.com.

Julie Kuliopulos was the call center manager for Braun during the process described in this case study. She is now a director of business development with Performix Technologies, a global leader in the delivery of solutions that improve the business performance of contact centers. With 10 years' experience in contact centers, she has helped a variety of international corporations dramatically improve service levels and reduce operating costs. Kuliopulos holds a master's degree in business administration from Suffolk University and a B.S. in business administration from Merrimack College. Additional education includes international studies at the University of London and Bocconi University in Milan, Italy, and Purdue University's Center for Customer Driven Quality, where she is also a guest speaker. Kuliopulos is co-author of "Surviving a Major Technology Change Over" published in *TeleProfessional*.

Natalie L. Petouhoff is the director of content for BenchmarkPortal. Her background ranges from technology to human resources. She has firsthand experience at companies such as General Electric, General Motors, Hughes Electronics, and Universal Studios as well as Internet start-up companies. She has a master's degree and a bachelor of metallurgical engineering degree from the University of Michigan.

Reference

Oakley, Ed, and Doug Krug. (1991). *Enlightened Leadership*. New York: Fireside Publishing.

Taking a Holistic Approach to Recruiting, Training, and Retention

Financial Services Company

Anne G. Nickerson and Elizabeth A. Ahearn

Three years ago Partners in Development and THE RADCLYFFE GROUP, under separate contracts, began work with the call center quality manager of a Fortune 500 financial services company to identify and implement a strategy to improve retention, increase customer sales and satisfaction, improve productivity, and raise morale. Partners in Development focused on the recruiting, screening, and hiring process; and THE RADCLYFFE GROUP focused on the training and performance management strategy. This case study outlines the steps we took to successfully meet those objectives, along with our lessons learned.

Introduction

The quality manager, a former training manager, had conducted a preliminary performance analysis and had identified high-level areas that required the focus of our consultant work. The manager's leadership, willingness to work with us on a business case for suggested changes, and ability to garner the support of the critical players in the organization increased our chance for success. She was also a firm believer in addressing the system as a whole, although she had aggressive and clear milestones of when results would need to be realized so she could continue to leverage the support of her senior management.

The company was experiencing an annual attrition rate of 60 percent, 20 percent of which was positive attrition into other parts of their company, with 38 percent of personnel leaving for jobs outside of the

This case was prepared to serve as a basis for discussion rather than to illustrate either effective or ineffective administrative and management practices. Names of places, organizations, or people have been disguised at the request of the author or organization.

company. Morale was at an all-time low and had recently been affected by realignment of departments and regions, change in senior management, and the advent of two new competing call centers within 10 miles of its primary call center site. Senior management wanted agents to move from a transaction role to more of a customer advocate role, with the ultimate goal of having 50 percent of its agents cross selling products. It was clear from the beginning that one of our deliverables would be a customized training program to meet the company's hiring demand, while integrating the training into new curriculum designed for an upgraded desktop interface. At the same time, we would work on ways to identify and feed the pool of candidates who had the customer service gene.

Our initial needs assessment identified these critical gaps:

- Critical competencies had not been identified nor had job descriptions been updated since before the reorganization.
- Recruiting and screening processes were not call center specific.
- Performance standards were not aligned to what was important to the customer.
- Myriad training programs from different areas were in use. The content was dependent on which subject matter expert was available to "train" the new hires. There were no validated assessments to test learning or performance.
- There was a monitoring process in place, but it was not introduced in training nor were managers calibrated and aligned on giving feedback.
- There was no specific recognition program in place to support the performance objectives.
- Work shifts were inflexible, and there was limited public transportation.

This case study outlines the solutions we implemented, the challenges that were faced, and results to date.

Recruiting
Building Competency Models and Job Descriptions

A job task analysis was available for the representative's position, but there was no competency model for hiring the representatives. We needed to align the job task analysis to a revised job description and then identify and map specific representatives' competencies. To accomplish this, we interviewed high and low performers who had at least 18 months' tenure, looked at the strategic direction of the company to uncover future competencies, and compiled industry research. We matched the competency profile with key behavioral descriptors. These served as the foundation of the recruiting profile, needs assessment survey, training objectives, performance standards, and evaluation of the effectiveness of the customer service training strategy. A partial example is illustrated in table 1.

Using this model, the call center managers identified a minimum set of skills and experiences that would be used to filter candidates out from the remaining hiring process. These skills and experiences

Table 1. Excerpt from customer service representative competency model.

Competency	Key Descriptors (How Demonstrated)
Customer focused and builds loyalty and confidence	• Is proactive in meeting customer needs • Provides information and resources • Uses good judgment in modifying policies and procedures • Follows up when promised • Is consultative when providing advice and direction
Empathizes	• Displays sensitivity to feelings • Recognizes and adjusts to unique needs • Remains calm and polite • Listens patiently without interrupting
Communicates effectively	• Asks appropriate questions • Speaks with clarity and good choice of words • Checks to test understanding • Expresses thoughts in writing that are logical, sequential, and customer focused • Uses correct grammar, sentence structure, spelling, and vocabulary
Problem solver	• Gathers available information and analyzes to arrive at appropriate resolution • Thinks through issues and implications before suggesting solutions • Applies logical reasoning to determine relationship of variables • Perceives patterns and problems that should be addressed to improve service
Organizes work activities	• Keeps information straight while handling several situations at once • Pays attention to details • Maintains accurate, complete, and up-to-date files on customer cases • Follows through on promised activities
Manages stress	• Controls emotions • Demonstrates tolerance, appropriate humor, and patience with irate or difficult customers • Answers same question repeatedly in pleasant, polite manner • Defuses hostility by acknowledging customer's feelings and responding with a can-do attitude

also were the core competencies used for later design and evaluation of the training program.

Executives at the firm quickly recognized our ability to find quality candidates who matched the profile and could fit the many full-time equivalent (FTE) seats that needed to be filled in this very competitive market.

The first program the call center HR team implemented was to offer current high performers an incentive to recruit candidates like themselves. High-performing customer service representatives (CSRs) received business cards to give to people in the community whom they met during their everyday activities and who appeared to have the right qualities for the job. For example, if a high performer was shopping in a mall and saw a clerk exhibiting the identified competencies, the "recruiter" would give the clerk a card and invite him or her to participate in the screening process.

High-performing recruiters would receive monetary rewards for each person they recruited who was hired. They would also get incremental monetary rewards for every three months that their candidate stayed on the job and met an 80 percent performance standard. This program proved to be one of the least expensive and most motivating programs for both the recruiter and candidate. More than half of the hired and retained candidates came through this program.

We then engaged the classified advertising and combined it with a voice response unit (VRU) automatic profiler to help find and screen additional candidates. The VRU profiler proved to be very efficient as an indicator, and we were also able to track which classifieds were pulling in the best candidates, thus spending those dollars more efficiently. The profiler asked a variety of questions, such as the following:

- Describe your highest level of education. For high school or GED diploma, press 1; for trade school, press 2; for associate's degree, press 3; for bachelor's degree and higher, press 4.
- Describe your number of years with customer service experience by selecting the number on the touch pad. If none, press 2.
- In what area of service do you have experience? For restaurant, press 1; for retail, press 2; for office, press 3; for other, press 4.
- Please listen carefully to a sample customer. At the sound of the tone, please record your reply.

Using the VRU, we eliminated hours of time originally spent reading resumes and scheduling candidates for interviews. Once a candidate completed the questions, the VRU scheduled any candidate who met our minimum qualifications for an interview within three days. We were able to reduce the time from advertisement to interview from three weeks to four days.

Finally, we added a job-posting icon to the corporate intranet and Internet, with an online application form. At the time, this took an enormous amount of coordination with the corporate technology team for very few users; however, we think that was due to the inexperience with the technology, both internally and externally. It is now more popular, and an effective mechanism to share available job postings throughout the organization.

Screening and Hiring

Once the eligible candidates had been identified, we set up three additional screenings before getting to the final interview: job applicant screening simulation, realistic job preview, and job aptitude test.

The job screening simulation is a computer-based program that presents sample customer calls and several potential responses. Candidates select the choices they feel are most representative of the best response, and their decisions are the basis for their scores. For example, the candidates would listen to a caller's issue, and their score would be determined on whether they selected an empathic response, accurately typed data in the proper fields, analyzed data in reference materials, and offered the caller appropriate information.

The realistic job preview was initially a presentation about job benefits that HR developed and presented, but we shifted to inviting current representatives to talk about their experiences for each prospective group of candidates. They described both what was great about the job and serving customers and what was difficult about the job. Their descriptions of the difficulties proved useful as candidates removed themselves from consideration if tales about irate callers and being tethered to the phone convinced them that the job was wrong for them. As call volume increased, we did not have consistent access to these representatives so we instead created a 15-minute videotape that illustrated a typical day and included their portion. This proved to be very successful in giving candidates a consistent message. It is now played just after the job simulation test, and offers the candidate an opportunity to self-select out of the hiring process because of inappropriate job fit.

Based on exit interview data of customer service representatives who either left the job or were asked to leave, we learned that one common theme among unsuccessful candidates was their lack of compassion for irate callers and inability to handle the high volume of calls. We also learned that the ability to think on one's feet and adjust to needs of the moment were critical. We then worked with a subcontracted vendor to create a prescreening application test to assess candidates' aptitude for the service environment, job ethics, writing and communication skills, and attention to detail and accuracy. Candidates took this test after the initial job simulation. It was an effective tool in separating those applicants who met the hiring objectives from those that exceeded the standards.

Initially, the top candidates who went through the job simulation had to wait one to two weeks before we invited them back for the aptitude test and interview. Several candidates that we liked had by then accepted a different job offer. We changed the process so we would not lose good candidates.

The revised process underwent a short pilot and was then adopted. We told candidates to expect the interview to last between two and three hours. Candidates spent approximately 90 minutes completing the simulation and viewing the videotape that demonstrates the job to them in real terms. They had to reach a minimum score on the simulation and respond with a grade of at least three on a scale of one to five to the question of whether they see this as a job fit. If they met the minimum qualifications, we asked them to take the aptitude test. If they met the minimum qualifications on the aptitude test, they were escorted to a room for a peer and manager interview.

Approximately five people began the process for every one job opening. Of those five, two candidates reached the interview stage. This percentage is a substantial win from the perspective of human resources, which conducts interviews.

Core interview teams conducted the final interviews. Each team included a high-performing representative and a hiring supervisor. The participants in the core interview team rotated and served as a beginning to a leadership development process. This approach often provided a balanced perspective of a candidate, both for job fit culture fit.

As we selected the core interview teams, we provided training in behavioral, or event based, interviewing skills. The premise of this approach is that past performance predicts future performance. We developed a consistent set of questions and follow-up questions for finding supporting information that the candidate has both the skills and values needed for the job.

Table 2 offers examples of behavioral questions used to identify proficiency in specific competencies.

Ranking

We had to identify the top potential candidates quickly so we had to find a way to tie the screening scores into a chart so that we could rank them. A spreadsheet was the easiest way to do this. Each screening tool had a score, which was then added and sorted from the highest to the lowest candidate. Table 3 illustrates the system. All scores were on a one-to-five scale, with one equal to low, and five to high.

Table 2. Excerpt from behavioral interview scoring chart.

Competency	Behavior Question	Notes/Score 1-5 (1=low; 5=high)
Customer focused and builds loyalty and confidence	Describe a time when you had to go above the call of duty. What was the situation, and what were your thoughts, actions, and the results?	
Problem solver	Give us an example of a time when someone asked you to answer a question you did not know the answer to. What did you do and what was the result?	
Empathizes	Walk us through an experience you had when someone you interacted with was very angry.	

Table 3. Example of the screening and hiring summary chart.

Candidate Name	Score: Job Simulation	Score: Job Aptitude	Score: Interview	Total Score:
Joe Smith	5	5	5	15
Alison Jones	5	4	4	13
John Johnson	4	4	4	12
Amelia Thompson	3	4	4	11

Training

The skills learned as a result of any kind of training should be integrated into behaviors that become part of the ongoing way of life in the organization, not an event. These new behaviors need to be reinforced in the work environment by leaders who consistently measure, coach, and model them. While nearly everyone agrees with this in concept, making it a reality is a completely different story.

In this case study, the client worked hard to ensure that training received the necessary resources and commitment so it would take hold. The *Fortune* 500 company's CEO earmarked the necessary dollars to successfully implement a performance improvement initiative. This initiative was truly "holistic," meaning that all aspects of the organization's people, processes, and systems were evaluated and integrated. A true measure of the CEO's belief, passion, and influence is that he attended the training. He could not only talk about the concepts and skills, but also model the behaviors in his interactions with his own clients, managers, and associates.

After development of the needs assessment and competency models, the team was ready to design a customized training. Most of the leadership and associates expected customer service training, but the CEO wanted the organization to deliver world-class service during every interaction with everyone in every circumstance. As the consultants, we ensured that the competencies originally designed in the model would provide the organization with the tangible skills to deliver this caliber of service consistently. The term *world-class service* has been the buzz phrase of the last decade, but few people have identified it in tangible terms and explained how world-class service gets translated from the corporation to each customer during an interaction. THE RADCLYFFE GROUP has, through research and focus groups, identified the specific world-class service characteristics that all customers want, and then we identified how to translate those characteristics into tangible behaviors performed during every interaction.

Performance Standards

Competency models had been developed for each function in the service organization. The holistic approach then continued with an integrated training plan that included both developing performance standards and measurements, against which the CSRs' behaviors would be measured. Since the client had already hired individuals who had the inherent abilities to perform the job, these individuals only needed refinement or development, or both, that would ensure a return-on-investment (ROI), which was being considered as a major success factor.

Competency models define inherent abilities of individuals and, within that, discrete skills and behavior that are tangible and can be easily measured. For each position within the service organization, performance standards need to be established so that CSRs know what it takes to meet the minimum requirements of the job and what it takes to exceed or perform above and beyond the minimum requirements of the job.

In terms of telephone performance, we developed a set of skills or behaviors and translated them onto an observation or monitoring form, as shown in figure 1. We also provided definitions of each performance standard and expectation. A performance standard is the minimum level of acceptable performance measured by either a "yes" or a "no" because this is a measurement of whether or not a behavior was performed. A performance expectation is a behavior performed based on skill level, knowledge, and experience and is a measurement of how well a behavior has been performed. Behaviors or skills can reside both in the standards and expectations category on the observation form.

Measurements and Performance Development Planning

Change is difficult for all associates and especially CSRs because it makes them feel out of control. As a result, it is always beneficial to involve them as much as possible in the process. Once the CSRs and leadership team attended the customized training and were aligned about the new behaviors required during each customer interaction, the CSRs performed a self-assessment of the required competencies (skills and behaviors) using the competency model form. The coaches then rated the CSRs' level of competency on the job using a form like that in table 4. Once the coaches completed these two assessments, a performance development plan that focused on methodical mastering of skills over time was developed for each individual. The coaches prepared a performance development plan that identified the skills that had been mastered within the last quarter, the skills on which to now focus, and the results that will be expected within the next quarter. This document identified specific skills, level of skill, and timeframe required to demonstrate consistent mastery of these skills in a real-work situation.

At this point the associates had specific, tangible skills on which to work, and they understood the measurement criteria, where they

Figure 1. Sample call observation form.

Sample Call Observation Form
THE RADCLYFFE GROUP, LLC

Associate _____ Caller _____

Coach _____ Call Number _____

Date of Coaching _____ Date of Call _____

Time of Coaching _____ Time of Call _____

Standards

Opening	(circle)			Comments/Key Notes/Words/Phrases
Used correct standard opening	Yes	No		
Acknowledged concern or compliment, when appropriate	Yes	No	N/A	
Gained control with an "I can" statement	Yes	No		
Transitioned to probing	Yes	No		

Body of Call	(circle)			Comments/Key Notes/Words/Phrases
Probed with situation, issue, and validation questions	Yes	No		
Explained why information was needed	Yes	No		
Let caller speak without interruption	Yes	No		
Gave accurate information	Yes	No		
Asked permission to put on hold	Yes	No	N/A	
Explained why hold was needed	Yes	No	N/A	
Thanked caller for holding	Yes	No	N/A	
Asked if caller had pen/paper	Yes	No	N/A	
Responded to all questions/comments	Yes	No		
Provided a solution with options	Yes	No		
Gained caller's acceptance	Yes	No		

Close	(circle)			Comments/Key Notes/Words/Phrases
Recapped information discussed	Yes	No		
Provided next steps	Yes	No		
Captured/confirmed daytime phone number	Yes	No	N/A	
Asked, "Is there anything else?"	Yes	No		
Transferred caller appropriately	Yes	No	N/A	
Thanked caller and closed call professionally	Yes	No		
Used caller's name appropriately	Yes	No		
Waited for caller to hang up first	Yes	No		

Legend
5 = World class
4 = Excellent
3 = Good
2 = Fair
1 = Unacceptable

Expectations	(circle)	Comments/Key Notes/Words/Phrases
Vocal tone and quality	1 2 3 4 5	
Explanation was understandable to caller	1 2 3 4 5	
Explanation was thorough	1 2 3 4 5	
Positioned information positively	1 2 3 4 5	
Conveyed value	1 2 3 4 5	
Identified business opportunities	1 2 3 4 5	

Coaching

What was the most critical behavior in this call?

Which type of coaching was given (circle one):

Praising   Refining   Redirecting   Deferred

Results of the coaching:

Comments

Overall Assessment

stood, and where they were headed. This knowledge alone was a morale booster and assisted in making the CSRs feel like professionals in business. They were being held accountable for personal and professional growth and development, and they were getting the attention and coaching needed to do so.

Table 4. Supporting the training initiative.

Standard	Definition	Purpose
Used correct standard opening	Included company name, associate's name, and an offer to help: "Thank you for calling TRG [THE RADCLYFFE GROUP]. This is Amy Smith. How may I help you?"	• Consistency. • Caller knows he or she has reached the right number. • Associate takes ownership of the call.
Acknowledged concern or compliment, when appropriate	Used a statement that indicated that the associate understood the caller's feelings and specifically how the situation affected the caller: "I understand how frustrating it must be to receive the wrong product in the mail."	• Gets caller to relax because the caller knows he or she has been heard. • Associate can begin to take control. • Associate does not need to apologize over and over. • Caller begins to perceive customized service.
Gained control with an "I can" statement	Included a strong positive statement to take ownership of the call: "I can help you with that"; "I'll be glad to look into that for you."	• Caller feels good because he or she knows he or she has reached someone who will own the issue. • Associate gets to repeat positive affirmation—improved sense of empowerment.
Transitioned to probing	Asked permission to probe and explained why the caller should answer questions: "So that I can resolve this as quickly as possible, may I ask you a few questions?"	• Caller will sit back and answer any questions the associate asks. • Caller verbally gives control of the call to the associate.

Performance development plans were initially developed using three sources of input:

- completed observation forms that included the performance standards and expectations
- self-assessments and the coaches' assessments, which mirror the competency model
- tracking and analysis documents that contain summary data from the individual observation forms.

Automatic call distributor (ACD) reports, which are collected from the call management system (CMS), which captures data from the phone system, are missing from the input sources at this point. Almost all call center organizations focus on quantitative metrics such as average handle time (AHT), the time it takes from start to finish to handle a customer's call, and after call work (ACW), the time it takes to wrap up or close a call after it has terminated with the customer. The ACD reports should be used only as a diagnostic tool for the coach to identify a potential issue. When coaches focus on ACD reports as the final result of success to CSRs, an inadvertent message gets sent that quantity is more important than quality. Coaches should use other means to isolate the core performance issue. If the coach focuses on performance and skill building, the numbers in the ACD reports will reflect that focus.

Performance development planning sessions, which are individualized for each CSR, are conducted quarterly and enable the CSR and the coach to see three things:
- where the CSR has been from a performance standards and expectations perspective
- where the CSR is right now from a performance standards and expectations perspective
- where the CSR is going in the next two to three months from a performance standards and expectations perspective.

The CSRs were pleased to see a clear direction for the future and how much they had achieved in the past few months in tangible terms.

University Style Curriculum

The first customized training that the CSRs received was in the workshop Strategic Interaction Skills, designed by THE RADCLYFFE GROUP. The leadership team participated independently of the CSRs in two workshops: Strategic Interaction Skills and Coaching for Service Quality.

Strategic Interaction Skills is a workshop designed using The Funnel Approach, a process that addresses adult learning principles also designed by THE RADCLYFFE GROUP. The Funnel Approach ensures that the participants learn from big picture to small and that they learn from a universal perspective to a situation- or company-specific perspective. This workshop is designed using THE RADCLYFFE GROUP's Group Discovery Process. In this process participants use activities, questions, or games, or any combination of the three, to reach conclusions and discover what they perceive as the truth, rather than receive information passively. This method effectively reduces the resistance facilitators often encounter when CSRs feel they already have the necessary skills to deliver world-class service.

In this workshop, the CSRs, through The Group Discovery Process, defined what world-class service is in tangible terms and then translated that into specific behaviors required in any call center. Those behaviors then translate into behaviors in their own environment, which then translate into their own calls with customers.

The CSRs learned to employ The Call Strategy, a process that includes a set of tangible skills that help the CSR navigate through the customer interaction effectively while delivering world-class service consistently. The Call Strategy has been tested and validated on more than 66,000 interactions to ensure that customers respond as predicted at least 98 percent of the time. Because the CSRs know that the steps of the strategy are likely to work 98 percent of the time, they become more confident and comfortable that they can control the customer interaction, not the customer.

Two months after implementing Strategic Interaction Skills and The Call Strategy (along with a holistic coaching program), the quality survey scores for the service experiences increased 10 points.

A university-style curriculum was then implemented to ensure ongoing development that enabled the client to implement a skills-based pay program. This program recognizes the CSRs for mastering new skills on an ongoing basis. A university-style curriculum is designed to motivate CSRs to complete a group of core courses and elective courses each within specific levels. Level 100 courses are basic workshops and require no previous training. Once the CSR has participated in each level 100 workshop required and passed the mastery testing, he or she can advance to level 200 courses, most of which have prerequisite level 100 workshops associated with them. Although three-quarters of the level 200 workshops are still considered part of the core curriculum, CSRs can begin to take elective courses to fulfill certification requirements. After the CSR has completed each level with mastery testing and has demonstrated proficiency back in the call center, he or she is eligible for an increase in pay on the basis of the newly obtained tangible skills.

Mentoring and Nesting

Once the seasoned staff was ready, the client implemented a mentoring program that provided new hires with mentors who provided them with coaching and guidance. This increased morale of the seasoned CSRs who were demonstrating the right behaviors and had shown significant consistency in demonstrating the new performance standards and expectations over time. Mentors received extra credit on their performance appraisals for taking on the responsibility and were eligible for an additional 2 percent on their merit increase.

When new hires graduate from their new hire class, they are immediately transferred to a new hire nest, which enables them to work together in a new hire team to handle their own split, or group, of calls. Their calls are specially routed to ensure that they are handling calls that will build their skills and their confidence in a methodical way.

Coaching

The coaching program was holistic as well. There are three major components to a successful coaching program:
- coaching skills development
- administration of coaching
- calibration.

Coaching Skills Development

Coaches, supervisors, trainers, managers, and directors need to be able to model two types of coaching for there to be a successful cultural change:
- *Immediate:* This is a step-by-step process for providing feedback in the moment that is either reinforcing the behavior or skill that one wants to continue, redirecting a nonexistent behavior or skill, or refining an existing behavior or skill.
- *Deferred:* This is a step-by-step process for providing feedback to individuals when immediate coaching has been performed and has been unsuccessful in behavioral change.

Each of these skills requires significant practice and requires that the coaches and leadership team be able to successfully identify performance standards and expectations during customer interactions. They need to be able to measure the performance standards and expectations against the specific criteria and complete the observation form accurately. Once the observation form is completed for the call, the coach needs to be able to name the behavior to be coached. Both immediate and deferred coaching skills are focused on:
- naming the specific behavior that was performed well or inadequately or was not existent
- providing the CSR with the result of the behavior that was performed well or inadequately or was absent

- providing a recommendation for continuation or improvement or asking for a recommendation
- gaining commitment to continue the behavior, improve the behavior, or include the behavior.

Administration of Coaching

An effective coaching program requires a level of commitment that is difficult to achieve but is well worth the effort because the results are so evident, both internally and externally.

We were successful with this client because the commitment to coaching was nonnegotiable. All barriers were removed once they were identified. Standards for immediate coaching were implemented, requiring coaches to monitor four CSR calls per week and provide immediate feedback. Since the average call length was no more than four minutes, it took, on average, five minutes to listen to a call for a specific behavior and provide immediate coaching using one of the three step-by-step coaching skills (reinforcing, refining, and redirecting). Because immediate coaching skills are designed to provide feedback in one direction only, coaches did not get bogged down in a lengthy discussion about the entire call.

Deferred coaching is performed twice a month for 30 minutes each. In this coaching, both the CSR and the coach assess recorded calls. The coach facilitates the discussions based on tangible performance standards and expectations (or behaviors) that either meet or do not meet specific criteria. The coach also focuses on call trends, helping the CSR to identify possible pitfalls on each call. At the end of this session, the CSR identifies the behavior for which he or she thinks the coach should provide support.

The standards of performance for coaching were fully integrated into the leaders' performance development plans, objectives, and performance appraisals. This set the expectation for the leadership team that its focus needed to be on coaching for performance improvement and success, not numbers.

By reviewing tracking and analysis documents and the reporting features of the recording system, senior leadership was able to assess whether the managers were holding each level accountable for its own standards of performance.

Calibration

Calibration is perhaps the most influential activity in the entire program. Calibration sessions are usually facilitated by an "expert" coach. The purpose of calibration is to keep coaches, supervisors, managers, and trainers aligned on how customer interactions are assessed equitably across the organization, within regions, and within teams. Calibration sessions help to develop the leaders' customer interaction skills, so that they are able to continue to develop the CSR skills with credibility and confidence. Additionally, it is critical to ensure consistency in feedback across all teams, so that the leadership team appears aligned on all aspects of the performance standards and expectations.

Calibration sessions focus on the pivotal behavior on the call, not only whether the standards and expectations have been met. These sessions create healthy discussion and debate and reduce the focus on a literal interpretation of the standards and expectations.

A pivotal behavior on a call may be the behavior that turned the call around or that behavior which, if performed differently, could have changed the outcome of the call. It is the behavior that had the most impact on the call. It is important to identify the pivotal behavior so that coaches can continue to focus on the bigger picture and provide CSRs with meaningful feedback, rather than nit-pick about behaviors that seem irrelevant to CSRs. During calibration sessions, preselected recorded calls are played and each coach completes an observation form, determining whether or not the standards were met and how well the expectations were achieved. The facilitator then leads a discussion with the primary goal of achieving group consensus. Once the group has discussed and agreed on whether or not the standards were met and how well the expectations were achieved, the facilitator leads a discussion to help the coaches identify the pivotal behavior on the call.

One of the biggest pitfalls in coaching programs is the lack of calibration sessions. When they do occur, the sessions are often ineffective because coaches are simply listening to calls and agreeing on whether a behavior was performed or not. The calibration sessions with this client were instrumental in the success of the coaching program because they were held to accomplish two things:
- staying focused on the philosophy behind the use of The Call Strategy—that is, meeting the customers' psychological and emotional needs
- ensuring that the coaches were able to come to a consensus on what is the behavior that had the most impact on the call outcome.

Conclusions

The Radclyffe Group's experience with the call center of a *Fortune* 500 financial services company proved to be successful by many measures. We were able to identify and implement a strategy to improve employee retention, satisfaction, productivity, and morale, while increasing customer sales.

The preliminary call center performance analysis identified areas requiring improvement. We worked with a management team committed to the change necessary to ensure success. We were able to customize a training program to meet its hiring demand, provide training for current CSRs to improve and maximize their strengths, and take advantage of their upgraded desktop interface.

Our initial needs assessment identified critical gaps in the existing processes of recruiting, screening and hiring, training, and coaching. Over a period of several months, we worked to address and eliminate these gaps by:

- identifying critical competencies and updating job descriptions to reflect reorganization changes
- improving recruiting and screening processes to be call center specific
- aligning performance standards to what was important to the customer
- streamlining and creating training materials to include validated assessments to test learning or performance for new hires
- redefining the monitoring process and calibrating managers to provide aligned feedback
- creating a recognition program to support performance objectives.

Questions for Discussion

1. What three things would you do differently when recruiting and hiring CSRs?
2. What three tangible action items can you put in place within the next month that will begin your move toward a more holistic approach to associate development?
3. What are the ways in which you can quantifiably demonstrate a return on the training investment?
4. What are three barriers you can anticipate when implementing changes to your hiring, training, or performance management process? What solutions can you think of to eliminate the barriers or get around them?
5. What support needs to be set up in order to coach you and your telephone and quality coaches, and to continuously develop leadership and management skills in your center?

The Authors

Anne G. Nickerson is principal founder of Call Center Coach, LLC, a firm that specializes in providing call center professionals with comprehensive developmental resources, such as Telephone Talk Show and Call Center Leadership and Mastery. In addition, Nickerson offers individualized one-on-one professional coaching. She is also the principal founder of Partners in Development, LLC, a human resources consulting firm that facilitates holistic and aligned human resource processes that support bottom-line business results.

Nickerson has more than 20 years' experience in organizational development, team building, facilitation, and customized training. She has specialized in customer service since 1995, with experience in recruiting, candidate screening, job selection processes, competency development, management and development, certification programs, developing performance standards and project management. During her career, she has held positions at Cornell Cooperative Extension and the University of Connecticut Continuing Education Department, and most recently she directed the Call Center People Renewal and Development function at CIGNA Corporation. She can be reached at 76 Kibbe Road, Ellington, CT 06029; email: anne@CallCenterCoach.com.

Elizabeth A. Ahearn is the president, CEO, and founder of THE RADCLYFFE GROUP, LLC, a firm located in Fairfield, New Jersey, and dedicated to helping clients deliver world-class service. Previously, Ahearn held call center leadership positions at Automatic Data Processing, IMS North America, the Pepsi-Cola Company, and Levi Strauss, where she was the recipient of both the Marketing Excellence Award and the Koshland Award for Outstanding Achievement.

Ahearn has served on the National Board of Directors for the Society of Consumer Affairs Professionals in Business (SOCAP) from 1993 to 2001. She is a member of the Institute of Management Consultants and the International Customer Service Association. She holds a master's degree from Seton Hall University and teaches at Purdue University's Call Center Campus, where she was the number one rated speaker in 2000 and 2001.

Findings From a Study on Selection Criteria for Higher Retention and Increased Productivity

Purdue University

Jon Anton and Anne G. Nickerson

The single biggest challenge that call center managers face today is finding enough people with the aptitudes and attitudes to handle the pressure of a constant stream of inbound and outbound telephone calls. Current hiring practices often result in annual turnover rates in excess of 100 percent, a very inefficient approach to the problem. The typical hiring process can be streamlined and result in the hiring of high-performing customer service representatives. This case study is based on data from over 500 call centers. It describes the specific preemployment screening processes that call center managers can implement to find people who will be a best fit for the job of customer service representatives.

Background

From studies conducted at Purdue University's Center for Customer-Driven Quality, where co-author Jon Anton is director of benchmark research, researchers estimate that in the United States alone there are more than 75,000 call centers staffed with more than three million customer service representatives (CSRs) handling in excess of 11 billion inbound and outbound calls annually (Anton, 1998, 1997, 1996, 1995). In our annual benchmark study of more than 500 call centers, their HR budget, as a percent of the total call center budget, averages a staggering 60 percent across all industries.

More important, the recruiting, screening, and training of new CSRs represents between 10 percent and 15 percent of the HR budget, and this amount is driven by an industrywide turnover rate of

This case was prepared to serve as a basis for discussion rather than to illustrate either effective or ineffective administrative and management practices.

from 30 percent to 100 percent per year. The message is simple: Many of the people hired to be CSRs do not really fit this line of work and quit because of lack of job satisfaction. Frequently, the job conditions and environment are excellent and the call center manager bears no responsibility. The person hired to be a CSR simply does not have the aptitude or attitude for the job.

The authors' experience in recruiting, screening, training, and monitoring CSRs leads us to believe that certain people have special talents for frontline telephone work and others do not. Those that have these special customer service "genes" (that is, fundamentally value resolving customer inquiries) do a better job on the telephone, are frequently happier with their work, and are exhilarated when they satisfy customers. They tend to stay longer in their positions, which leads to lower turnover. By contrast, those people who do not have these customer service genes tend not to like their jobs, find servicing customers exhausting, and leave their positions much more quickly.

It becomes more difficult for companies to hire and retain the best CSRs during a tight job market, when they undertake thorough backgrounds checks, and when the training requirements are complex.

Companies may find the cost of hiring a CSR shockingly expensive. The total hiring costs include recruiting, screening, and testing as well as training to enable a new hire to handle calls completely and independently. Table 1 shows the costs involved for hiring one CSR in four categories, according to the Purdue Benchmark Report.

Table 1. Cost of hiring CSRs.

CSR Level	Description	Costs Reported
One	Simple where to buy, order taking, where to fix, and call routing	$5,000
Two	Consumer affairs, i.e., complaint handling	$8,000
Three	Technical support problem solving	$12,000
Four	Professionals, such as nurses or stock brokers	$18,000

To solve this problem, call center managers have worked closely with the industry to develop and validate job applicant screening processes. The current availability of these thorough screening techniques for CSR job applicants is producing results and increasing the probability of finding the right person for the job, thereby reducing needless and expensive turnover. The authors have conducted an exhaustive study of the types of screening processes that exist today. They are as follows:

- interactive voice recognition (IVR) resume profiling
- telephone voice assessment
- aptitude testing and job fit analysis
- job previews
- realistic job simulations
- live interviews
- telephone role plays
- background checking.

In the subsequent sections of this article, we will describe each of these methods and give the reader some idea of the cost and effectiveness of each.

Core Competencies

The job screening process that the industry has developed requires that companies apply strict standards of proof to demonstrate that screening tests reflect the applicable jobs. To ensure that the tests match the jobs, companies must first identify the components of the job. Then they can develop a test to assess applicants' ability to handle it. The core competencies that are part of a CSR's job include the following:

- simultaneously thinks, talks, and types
- listens with empathy
- is attentive to details
- expresses ideas clearly
- is a problem solver.

After a manager has identified the core competencies, he or she would integrate them into the screening process. Following are descriptions of the types of screening processes now available.

IVR Resume Profiling

DESCRIPTION. The first step in any CSR recruitment process is often the placement of a job advertisement in the classified section of a local newspaper or a professional magazine. The advertisement normally asks the job applicant to send a resume describing his or her background and experiences that match the job description.

IVR resume profiling is a method several companies offer to streamline this recruiting process. The process typically includes the following services:

- The companies help writing and placing the job ad, putting a focus on saying very little except to call a toll free number for more details.
- The companies' interactive voice recognition units answer the job applicant calls.
- The companies' IVR script guides job applicants through a series of questions that are specifically designed to screen their education and work experience to best fit the CSR job description.
- The companies may customize prequalifying criteria, such as matching for job fit, availability for shifts, or willingness to submit to a drug screen.
- If there is a good match between a job applicant's responses to the IVR and the profile required for the job, the IVR encourages the applicant to select from a list of possible interview times.
- The service gives its client a list of all applicants and ranks them from best fit to worst fit.
- The service also prepares a market analysis to show the client which newspapers pulled more calls and the geographic profile of the respondents' locations.
- Several vendors now supply the data immediately through a pass code–protected Website.

COST. From interviews with vendors, the authors found that the service costs between $2 and $8 per CSR selected.

CURRENT USAGE. The Purdue Benchmark Report for all industries found that only 6 percent of the reporting call centers use IVR resume profiling to screen job applicants. We interviewed a number of companies that use this type of service and found they were very satisfied with the results and extremely positive about the payback of money and time invested on it. Companies stated that an overwhelming advantage was that candidates could respond whenever they were available and be scheduled the day following the ad placement, saving valuable time and resources. One company reported that it reduced time from advertising to interview from three weeks to one day. Others said a plus to this technology was the ease of identifying qualifying candidates before the interview and automatically setting up confirmed interview schedules.

Telephone Voice Assessment

DESCRIPTION. Once an applicant with the required education and work experience for a CSR job opening has been located by a review of resumes or use of an IVR resume profiling system, many companies conduct a telephone voice assessment of the applicant. One of the core competencies for the CSR job in many companies is proper projection on the telephone and certain features of tone and volume. HR professionals may conduct this process internally or outsource it to specialty companies.

COST. The telephone voice assessment costs between $4 and $10 per applicant interview, depending on the extent of the interview.

CURRENT USAGE. In the Purdue Benchmark Report for all industries, 52 percent of the reporting call centers used telephone voice assessment services to screen job applicants. Internal HR staff conduct most of these interviews, not outside service companies. Companies that routinely do preemployment telephone voice assessment said they were convinced telephone communication is the most important skill of a CSR. Therefore, voice tone, volume, and personality are critical for influencing caller satisfaction.

Aptitude Testing

DESCRIPTION. The concept of aptitude testing is prevalent throughout most industries. Its recent adoption by call centers is a logical extension of the theory that people have different aptitudes for job skills and that this testing can be used for applicant selection purposes. These tests are often used to determine if candidates have the customer service genes. The core competencies might include the customer service genes—that is, that the candidate fundamentally values resolving customer inquiries—as well as skills in math, logic, or whatever is needed for a specific job. To measure interpersonal skills, for example, the test might ask a candidate his or her likes and dislikes for certain tasks on a scale of one to 10. If accuracy and attention to detail are important, it might ask a candidate to compare similar documents and identify inaccuracies. Most of these tests can be completed either online or offline.

COST. The study showed that the cost varied from a low of $35 per test to a high of $100 per test. The variation seemed to be with the level of self-service in adapting and conducting the testing procedure as well as with the level of computerization of the results.

CURRENT USAGE. The Purdue report found that 32 percent of the call centers used aptitude testing to screen job applicants. No one company had developed an aptitude test exclusively for call center CSRs, but several companies specialize in offering CSR-specific aptitude tests.

Companies that used even standard aptitude tests were quite pleased with the results and planned to expand these activities in the future.

Job Preview

DESCRIPTION. A job preview is a way to give a job candidate a taste of the job under consideration. When candidates consider whether they are interested in a job, they have numerous questions about job fit, such as skills required, types of clients they will interact with, benefits, training requirements, how family friendly the company is, and what development opportunities exist and are supported. Companies often present candidates with this information so they will know the reality of the job and be better able to assess whether the company would be the right choice or wrong choice for them. Some companies invite candidates to preview the job by spending a day at their site. That may not be possible for companies with larger multiple sites or in which confidential information is accessible on computer screens. A multimedia solution is often the answer for them.

COST. The costs associated with job previews vary with the approach and medium. From our interviews, the cost was as low as $250 for a desktop-published brochure to over $20,000 for a multimedia video and graphic display about the job.

CURRENT USAGE. Of the companies interviewed, 90 percent indicated they offered written job preview information. Over 38 percent indicated that they initially invested over $15,000 on multimedia presentations, realizing a return very quickly through consistency of image, message, and deselection (that is, removal from job consideration) by candidates themselves.

Realistic Job Simulation

DESCRIPTION. The most common realistic job preview occurs when a job applicant is asked to observe an experienced CSR taking telephone calls. The main flaw in this approach is simple: Experienced CSRs enjoy the job, are excellent at it, and make it look easy and enjoyable. The core competencies the job simulation preview assesses are listening, learning, remembering, and typing.

A second approach involves simulating the CSR's job. The applicant spends one to two hours in a cubicle similar to those of CSRs, listening to and responding to phone calls that are designed to sound authentic but have been generated by computer for this screening test. The job applicant simulation screening system, also known as JASS, monitors every response and compares each applicant to a database of top CSRs.

In the process, the applicant and the company can compare performance on issues like listening, typing, accuracy, learning, problem solving, and logic. It becomes immediately clear which applicants have the natural skills for this type of work and which do not. Applicants deselect themselves once they are exposed to a realistic job simulation of a CSR's seven to eight-hour day.

COST. The realistic job simulation, simulated by PC-based computer hardware and software, is a relatively new product. Currently the price per applicant screening ranges from $10 to $30 depending upon the volume of applicants screened. Some software can be purchased as a site license or as a corporate license depending upon the number of call centers involved, and per user for smaller call centers.

CURRENT USAGE. The Purdue report found that 29 percent of the reporting call centers used realistic job simulations to screen job applicants. Almost all of these were the type in which job applicants observe and listen to competent agents handling calls. This type of job simulation does not allow applicants to experience the pressures of the job and may result in CSRs leaving their positions after they experience the rigors of the job and all its requirements. We have talked to more than 20 companies that use a fully simulated CSR calling experience to give applicants a realistic job simulation. These companies report having tremendous success in properly exposing the applicant to the CSR job in a most realistic fashion. By a combination of applicant deselection and selection of only those applicants that score high on the job preview, these companies are reducing turnover and saving thousands of dollars in the process. We have found that this process can cut turnover by 11 percent.

Live Interviews

DESCRIPTION. Live interviews need almost no explanation. We all do live interviews in the recruiting process. There are well-documented steps to making live interviews a truly quantitative process, and this is not the topic of this case study. Suffice it to say that a written script (so that all interviews say the same thing to the applicant), using past experiences to predict future performance, and an evaluation matrix can make this process consistent and predictive of potentially high performers. The core competencies the live interview assesses are articulation, listening, negotiating, stress management, and voice tone and volume.

We all also know that live interviews are time-consuming for managers at all levels and that proper screening for only the best applicants can substantially reduce management time spent on this process.

COST. When the costs associated with a manager's time are taken into consideration, live interviews can easily cost from $30 to $60 per applicant, especially when each applicant may have to be interviewed by several levels of management.

CURRENT USAGE. The Purdue report found that 95 percent of the reporting call centers use live interviews to screen job applicants. Live interviews will always be an important part of the screening process.

Telephone Role Plays

DESCRIPTION. For CSRs who also have extensive professional training (such as nurses, doctors, lawyers, and brokers), telephone role plays may be the one additional step to take before offering employment. The core competencies this role play assesses are articulation, extemporaneousness, empathy, and creativity.

Companies specialize in conducting strategically designed telephone role plays with these professional job applicants. A trained industrial psychologist conducts the telephone call, listening carefully to every aspect of the applicant's responses and evaluating him or her on both form and content.

COST. The cost of telephone role plays varies considerably, but it is always expensive. Depending on the critical nature of the job, the costs range from $100 to $400 per applicant.

CURRENT USAGE. In the Purdue Benchmark Report for all industries, only 2 percent of the reporting call centers use telephone role plays to screen job applicants. If one considers only the call centers staffed by professionals, this utilization can increase to over 50 percent.

Companies using professional industrial psychologists for telephone role plays have been very satisfied with the quality of the results.

Background Checks

DESCRIPTION. As the risks of negligent hiring grow, there has been an increased demand for quick and accurate background checks into public records to verify information applicants have provided about their criminal record, credit history, education, and employment. HR professionals can undertake these checks internally, or they can be outsourced to companies that specialize in tracking, obtaining, and verifying public records. The core competencies background checks assess are honesty, attendance, work attitude, and work aptitude.

COST. The cost of background checks varies by the number of options requested for the search and whether or not specific searches link to live databases as part of the package. Vendor prices usually represent a set-up charge for software, and per applicant charges range from $20 to $100, depending on the state, information availability, and method of processing verification. Costs increase with requests for additional and more in-depth searches.

CURRENT USAGE. Companies are spending $3 billion annually on background checks. Of the companies we interviewed, 40 percent are using background checks as a part of their screening process. Of those doing background checks, 75 percent have contracted external vendors to secure this information.

Validation of Screening Processes

The proper validation of any job applicant screening process is a critical phase in the product design. The highest level of design importance in any screening process is to ensure that there is no built-in bias based on gender, ethnicity, or possible cultural issues.

The job analysis must match the screening tool measures. Likewise, the content of any test must represent the job competencies, and a statistical process must be employed to establish and demonstrate a relationship between test scores and job performance. Any selection system needs to abide by the recommended uses of the screening test, and stringent attention must be given to administrative instructions.

Return-on-Investment Considerations

Most management decisions related to appropriating corporate funds for new initiatives are driven by a forecasted payback, or return-on-investment (ROI) calculation. Obviously, the higher the ROI, the greater is the likelihood that a company will spend the money to correct a problem (Anton, Monger, and Perkins, 1997).

When preparing an ROI calculation for a job applicant screening initiative, managers should evaluate the following:
- To what degree can turnover be reduced?
- What is reduced turnover worth?
- What is the reduction in management time when thorough pre-interview screening has been completed?

Let us analyze one example of a call center experiencing 40 percent turnover in CSRs. Assume 100 CSR seats must be filled to operate this call center. Using our industry average for estimating the annual call center budget, we multiply $100,000 (the average for all industries of call center budget divided by the number of full-time equivalents) by the number of full-time CSRs. With this assumption, the annual budget for this hypothetical call center is $10 million.

Using our figure that the HR budget is 60 percent of the total annual budget and that recruiting, screening, and training (that is, the turnover cost) are approximately 10 percent of the 60 percent, we determine that turnover is currently costing this call center $600,000 per year.

Therefore, if we invested $150,000 in a realistic job preview screening tool and turnover was reduced 25 percent (from 40 percent to 30 percent), we would save $150,000 in the first year. Logically then, the ROI would be 100 percent in one year. In this case, this would be very sound corporate investment.

Conclusions

Screening works well when properly applied to job applicants considering employment in a call center. The Purdue Benchmark Report research shows that we have been able to observe the following results:
- Proper screening reduces the cost to add a new CSR.
- Proper screening reduces costly CSR turnover.
- Proper screening assures profit, thus keeps employee motivation and morale in a positive direction.
- Lower CSR turnover increases caller satisfaction.
- Lower CSR turnover reduces the cost per call.

Questions for Discussion
1. What are the costs of hiring a CSR?
2. How much of the HR budget is spent on hiring?
3. What is the ROI if tools are used for hiring?
4. What are eight tools that can help hiring managers?
5. How does properly screening a candidate help both the call center agent and the call center manager in deciding if the candidate and the job are a good fit?

The Authors

Jon Anton is the director of benchmark research at Purdue University's Center for Customer-Driven Quality. He specializes in enhancing customer service strategy through inbound call centers and e-business centers, using the latest in telecommunications (voice) and computer (digital) technology. He has been the principal investigator of the annual Purdue University Call Center Benchmark Research Report. Anton has developed techniques for calculating the ROI for customer service initiatives and has assisted over 400 companies. Based on the analysis of this data, Anton is the author of "The Purdue Page" in *Call Center Magazine* each month, plus the "Dr. Jon Benchmarks" in *Call Center News* each month. In October 2000, Anton was named to the Call Center Hall of Fame. In January 2001, he was selected for the industry's Leaders and Legends Award by *Help Desk 2000*. He has published 75 papers and seven professional books on customer service and call center methods in industry journals. He can be reached at 1532 South Campus Courts-E, Purdue University, Lafayette, IN 47907; 805.934.1004, extension 18; email: drjonanton@benchmarkportal.com.

Anne G. Nickerson is principal founder of Call Center Coach, LLC, a firm that specializes in providing call center professionals with comprehensive developmental resources, such as Telephone Talk Show and Call Center Leadership and Mastery. In addition, Nickerson offers individualized one-on-one professional coaching. She is also the principal founder of Partners in Development, LLC, a human resources consulting firm that facilitates holistic and aligned human resource processes that support bottom-line business results.

Nickerson has more than 20 years' experience in organizational development, team building, facilitation, and customized training. She has specialized in customer service since 1995, with experience in recruiting, candidate screening, job selection processes, competency development, management and development, certification programs, developing performance standards, and project management. During her career, she has held positions at Cornell Cooperative Extension and the University of Connecticut Continuing Education Department, and most recently she directed the Call Center People Renewal and Development function at CIGNA Corporation.

References

Anton, Jon. (1995, 1996, 1997, 1998). *Call Center Benchmark Reports*. West Lafayette, IN: BenchmarkPortal.

Anton, Jon, Jodie Monger, and Debra Perkins. (1997). *Call Center Management by the Numbers*. West Lafayette, IN: Purdue University Press.

About the Editor

Natalie L. Petouhoff works as a principal investigator with Jon Anton, who is director of benchmark research at Purdue University's Center for Customer-Driven Quality. She creates articles, books, and white papers that provide companies mission-critical information to enhance their customer service strategy through inbound call and e-business centers using the latest in telecommunications (voice) and computer (digital) technology. Petouhoff also specializes in using the Internet for external customer access as well as intranets and middleware. In addition, she is a partner at LMR associates where she specializes in return-on-investment (ROI) for "soft skills" and is a program manager for change management program as well as a trainer of work style behavior change.

Petouhoff's background ranges from technology (where she did basic scientific research to working on the manufacturing floor) to reengineering human resources, including programs in recruiting, training, leadership, integrated product, business process reengineering, coaching, and mentoring. She has firsthand experience at General Electric, General Motors, Hughes Electronics, Universal Studios, and other long-established companies as well as at Internet start-up companies. She believes that customer call centers are the ambassadors of a company, as they are generally one of the first places in a business that customers encounter. Her signature speech, "No People, No Business," demonstrates her commitment to helping companies understand the value of the human asset when benchmarking.

As a former change management consultant for Pricewaterhouse-Coopers, Petouhoff evaluated and installed call centers and enterprise resource planning (ERP) systems, and designed customer access interfaces. Through this frontline experience at companies like Warner Lambert and Sony Pictures Entertainment, she was able see the challenges companies face when implementing new technology solutions and changing workflow processes.

Petouhoff is currently working on a human potential ROI calculator. This will help companies see the value of training and developing employees as well as provide a way to quantify human capital as a corporate asset. Petouhoff has come up with a credible way to calculate how the degree to which people accept change can allow for the full return on investment for expensive technology. She also specializes in helping companies reduce the employee resistance that always accompanies change.

For her outstanding work in technology at Hughes Electronics, she received three awards: the Leadership Achievement Award for leadership in the face of resistance, the Superior Management Award for quick technology solution implementation with a tiger team, and the Peer-Selected Award for demonstrating exemplary behavior toward peers.

Natalie Petouhoff has published 10 technical papers in industry journals. She is a popular speaker as evidenced by being asked to speak at the Women and Technology Conference in Santa Clara to an audience of over 6,000 technical women about her latest ideas in technology as applied to customer service and career development.

Petouhoff's formal education is in technology. She was awarded the General Motors Fellowship to complete her doctorate of engineering from UCLA where she did her thesis research at Oak Ridge National Laboratory and Hughes Research Laboratories in metallurgy and high energy particle physics. She has master's and bachelor's degrees in metallurgical engineering from the University of Michigan financed by five scholarships. She can be reached at 3130 Skyway, Suite 702, Santa Maria, CA 93455; email: nataliepetouhoff@benchmarkportal.com.

About the Series Editor

J ack J. Phillips is a world-renowned expert on measurement and
evaluation and developer of the ROI process, a revolutionary process
that provides bottom-line figures and accountability for all types
of training, performance improvement, human resources, and technology programs.

He is the author or editor of more than 20 books—eight focused
on measurement and evaluation—and more than 100 articles.

His expertise in measurement and evaluation is based on more
than 27 years of corporate experience in five industries (aerospace,
textiles, metals, construction materials, and banking). Phillips has served
as training and development manager at two *Fortune* 500 firms, senior
HR officer at two firms, president of a regional federal savings bank,
and management professor at a major state university.

In 1992, Phillips founded Performance Resources Organization
(PRO), an international consulting firm that provides comprehensive
assessment, measurement, and evaluation services for organizations.
In 1999, the Franklin Covey Company purchased PRO, and it is now
known as the Jack Phillips Center for Research. Today it is an independent, leading provider of measurement and evaluation services to
the global business community. Phillips consults with clients in manufacturing, service, and government organizations in the United States,
Canada, Sweden, England, Belgium, Germany, Italy, Holland, South
Africa, Mexico, Venezuela, Malaysia, Indonesia, Hong Kong, Australia,
New Zealand, and Singapore. He leads the Phillips Center in research
and publishing efforts that support the knowledge and development
of assessment, measurement, and evaluation.

Phillips's most recent books include *The Human Resources Scorecard: Measuring the Return on Investment* (Boston: Butterworth-Heinemann, 2001); *The Consultant's Scorecard* (New York: McGraw-Hill,
2000); *HRD Trends Worldwide: Shared Solutions to Compete in a Global
Economy* (Boston: Butterworth-Heinemann, previously published by Gulf
Publishing); *Return on Investment in Training and Performance Improvement Programs* (Boston: Butterworth-Heinemann, previously published

by Gulf Publishing, 1997); *Handbook of Training Evaluation and Measurement Methods,* 3d edition (Boston: Butterworth-Heinemann, previously published by Gulf Publishing, 1997); and *Accountability in Human Resource Management* (Butterworth-Heinemann, previously published by Gulf Publishing, 1996).

Phillips has undergraduate degrees in electrical engineering, physics, and mathematics from Southern Polytechnic State University and Oglethorpe University, a master's degree in decision sciences from Georgia State University, and a Ph.D. in human resource management from the University of Alabama. In 1987 he won the Yoder-Heneman Personnel Creative Application Award from the Society for Human Resource Management.

Phillips can be reached at The Jack Phillips Center for Research, P.O. Box 380637, Birmingham, AL 35238-0637; phone: 205.678.8038; fax: 205.678.0177; email: serieseditor@aol.com.